GROUND RULES
IN PSYCHOTHERAPY
AND COUNSELLING

Robert Langs

GROUND RULES
IN PSYCHOTHERAPY
AND COUNSELLING

Robert Langs

London
KARNAC BOOKS

First published in 1998 by
H. Karnac (Books) Ltd.
58 Gloucester Road
London SW7 4QY

British Library Cataloging in Publication Data

A C.I.P. record for this book is available from the British Library.

ISBN 1 85575 171 2

Edited, designed, and produced by Communication Crafts

Printed in Great Britain by BPCC Wheatons Ltd, Exeter

10 9 8 7 6 5 4 3 2 1

I am indebted once again to James Raney, M.D.,
who, with great sensitivity and acumen, edited this book

CONTENTS

PART ONE

THE UNIVERSAL ATTRIBUTES OF THERAPY FRAMES

CHAPTER ONE

Nature framing nature

Throughout the history of the universe, frames, contexts, rules, and boundaries have been vital aspects of the development and very existence of both physical structures and living organisms (deDuve, 1995; Langs, 1996).

On the material side, both large and infinitely small entities are bounded, defined contextually, and constrained by rules and regularities. The most basic set of rules take form as the *laws* of nature that give the universe its determinism and predictability, chaotic and otherwise. Even quantum-related events, which apply to the fundamental particles of nature and have an ultimate degree of uncertainty, are nevertheless lawful.

The consistencies and certainties defined by rules and laws are buttressed by the physical *boundaries* that define material conglomerates. Boundaries have also played a vital role in the evolution of the universe. It was, for example, the bounding of a chaotic mass of energy and matter that created the earth some 10 billion years ago. On all levels of physical organization, then, order is the essential grounding for disorder, development, evolution, creativity, and the emergence of new forms (Langs, Bada-lamenti, & Thomson, 1996; Prigogine & Stengers, 1984).

As for living organisms, contexts, frames, rules, and laws have governed their development, functions, activities, and adaptations from the first moment of their emergence. On the most fundamental level, organisms are governed by the physical laws of nature and, in addition, by regularities and patterns that are uniquely characteristic of biological processes. As organisms move up the evolutionary scale and become increasingly complex, instinctive and then consciously fashioned rules of behaviour and coping have been forged as supplements to the natural laws on which they are grounded. Here, too, *contextual order* is essential for both smooth functioning and organismic development.

In humans, rules and laws of behaviour and conduct, moral and otherwise, govern actions and interactions with others. Taking form both explicitly and implicitly, these rules are fashioned and reshaped under the influence of both conscious and unconscious needs and forces. Rules are essential to the creation of a relatively stable and predictable environment of a kind that sustains life, protects an individual from harm, and supports adaptive efforts—rules define and safeguard self, relationships with others, and interpersonal transactions. Every situation and relationship that an individual comes upon is affected by a contextual set of biologically, socially, and individually determined ground rules. Humans also have the capability of choosing, consciously and/or unconsciously, to adhere to or violate these rules, doing so under considerable unconscious influence.

With respect to *boundaries*, biological boundaries or borders define and afford separate identity to a vast panoply of microscopic and macroscopic organisms. Boundaries stand as vital lines of contact between whatever lies within an organism and whatever lies outside it. These defining edges exist *within* entities and delineate their components, as well as *between* entities and their *environments*, which include physical features and other living beings. The importance of boundaries is seen, for example, in the fact that the creation of the cell boundary was the essential emergent event that enabled life to materialize some 4 billion years ago from the unbounded chemical soup that was its matrix. Indeed, the preservation of this same boundary is a *sine qua non* for a cell's survival.

In living beings, boundaries are by no means inert or passive: they are extremely active sites. They operate as highly selective and influential envelopes and membranes that are the locus of life-sustaining incorporative and excretory metabolic and other activities. In higher organisms, the proper management of boundary conditions and transactions is critical for successful adaptation and survival. Boundary conditions also affect the status and operations of the elements and entities within their confines. The properties of boundaries are of such great import that their measurement yields decisive information about the operations and state of the systems that they contain. In living organisms, boundaries define, regulate, and shape the activities that transpire within their territories.

Because they function as both borders and sites of critical metabolic processes, boundaries defy the usual distinctions between figure and ground, container and contained, defining structure and operational component. They are both the context for adaptation and adaptational entities themselves. In addition, they serve to keep an organism both separate from and merged with its environment. For humans, boundaries have both physical and psychological features—intrapsychic and interpersonal. The importance of boundaries for living entities cannot be overestimated.

Contexts, frames, and frameworks are terms that refer broadly to the conditions within and under which living organisms exist, function, relate, and adapt. Context is the broader term in that it refers to the physical and psychological circumstances of existing and interacting, including historical aspects, role definitions, rules, and other conditional features. Frames are contexts that can be altered and managed through framing activities and interventions.

Contexts and frames may be relatively fixed or in flux and changing, as seen when a couple moves from a friendship to an engagement to a marriage. As both physical settings and emotionally charged, psychological configurations, contexts and frames provide definitive, environmentally relevant background information and meaning—*contextual or interactive meaning*—to foreground thinking, behaving, and adapting. But framing activities also constitute adaptive actions that are rich in emotionally meaningful qualities of their own. These attributes are evident, for example, when a crime is committed—the rule violation serves to frame the relationship between the thief and the victim, while the theft itself is a framing action fraught with conscious and unconscious meanings—an active adaptation-evoking trigger that elicits further efforts at adaptation by both parties to the situation.

Contexts and frames activate and define organismic responses that cannot be properly understood without knowledge of these conditional factors. In substance, then, contexts and frames speak for *the conditional and relative nature of all human experience.*

Frames and frameworks are contexts that tend to be relatively well defined and stable, though subject to change as well. Frames mark off the spatial, temporal, interpersonal, and intrapsychic aspects of both physical and psychological structures, processes, and events. They include rules, laws, and contracts; the definition of roles and responsibilities; limits and constraints; expectations and acceptable behaviours and responses; settings; and the historical elements of a given relationship and interaction.

Framing activities or managing the setting and ground rules form a broad group of functions that are carried out by means of establishing a physical space and a set of rules and boundaries for a given relationship or interaction. While psychological and interpersonal frames may be rather stable and relatively unchanging, frames are rarely static but are usually in a state of flux. Framing creates conditions for human interactions not unlike dramatic stage settings that have both fixed and movable features, and which also may at times be the main issue for the action of the play.

Stable, secured frames tend to be safe and inherently supportive, while *unstable, insecure frames* tend to be disruptive and harmful. Insecure frames create states of disequilibrium and dysfunction to the point where they tend to become the primary concern of those who are under their influence. Because the frame is more fundamental and affecting than the actions it contextualizes, dealing with frame issues, usually by stabilizing the frame, is an adaptive task that takes precedence over dealing with other concerns that cannot be dealt with and resolved effectively without a secured frame.

For humans, a sound frame acts as a safe and supportive, highly stable backdrop and container for coping and surviving. Nevertheless, secured frames are also suffused with constraints and limitations that afford them entrapping qualities that create an unusual type of intensely disruptive anxiety—*existential death anxiety*. This sense of confinement is linked to the entrapping qualities of human existence itself—the gift of life that must end in death (Langs, 1997).

In contrast, unstable and insecure frames are damaging and unconsciously arouse another form of death anxiety—*predatory death anxiety* (Langs, 1997). This type of anxiety tends to be experienced unconsciously and greatly affects both behaviour and emotional state. However, modified and uncertain frames also offer maladaptive defences against the far more dreaded (yet invaluable) secured frame and the existential anxieties that it arouses. Thus, for humans, both secured and compromised frames and framing efforts have mixed effects, although *in toto*, a secured frame serves as a far more supportive and constructive context for human interactions and adaptations than does the far more costly and perilous modified frame.

Contexts for frames and framing

There are two additional perspectives that can help us to understand and appreciate the role of ground rules and boundaries in the psychotherapy process. The first involves the recognition of three major factors in human emotional adaptation.

1. *The need for safety, care, and holding.* Basic personal human resources such as a stable personality, a sound capacity for self-regulation, the ability to sustain emotional equilibrium, and the development of effective adaptive capabilities require stable and safe relationships and settings; proper care and support; stimulation for growth and development; and a variety of other positive experiences and affiliations. The necessity for this empathic and compassionate climate has been stressed by a wide

range of interpersonally oriented theorists (Langs, 1988)—to the relative exclusion, however, of the other two factors that shape emotional life.

2. *The experience of trauma.* While support is essential for the development and use of adaptive resources, *traumatic events are the ultimate test of these capabilities.* In addition, traumatic experiences tend to reshape the configuration and operations of adaptive assets, enhancing some aspects while seriously, and at times, permanently damaging others. If we define traumas in terms of the adaptational load that they place on the emotional mind, these range from minor incidents to those experiences that overload the psychic apparatus and cause adaptational malfunctions.

Emotional overload has many sources, ranging from major catastrophes like the death of a loved one to the slow accumulation of less intense but disruptive impingements. By and large, overload prompts the automatic invocation of denial-based, obliterating defences, and in many cases they become an essential feature of an individual's favoured mode of adaptation to emotionally charged events. All in all, the experience of trauma plays a significant role in the emotional life of all humans; dealing with trauma is the crucial test of emotionally related resources.

3. *The nature of frames and framing activities.* The final factor— and, of course, all three factors are interrelated—pertains to frames and framing activities that affect emotional adaptations in several ways. Frames are, as noted, the influential contexts for both development and adaptation. Secured frames support these processes, while modified frames impede them. Although it is conceivable that, for example, a parent could be fully supportive in a frame-modified home setting, the rule is that deviant frames, poor caring, and frequent traumas tend to go hand in hand. In addition, every major trauma involves some kind of frame violation, while every frame violation is a traumatic experience. Frames also contribute to the experienced meanings of traumas and to how an individual copes with them. *Indeed, a person's basic mode of adaptation is, at its core, either frame-securing (adhering to rules and boundaries) or frame-modifying (breaking rules and violating boundaries).*

In all, then, frames take their place along with nurturance and trauma as the main determinants of the vicissitudes of emotional life.

The second perspective on frames and framing activities involves a clarification of the essences of emotional life itself. There has been, of late, a rush of effort to define more clearly the psychological and physical aspects of human emotions, with a concentration on *acute emotional states* (e.g. Goleman, 1995; LeDoux, 1996; Plutchik, 1993). Less explored and barely understood are the residuals of these intense emotional moments and their subsequent working over—the mental (and bodily) processing of emotionally charged impingements and the information and meaning that they embody. The distinction between acute emotional states and their subsequent processing is of some importance for the perspectives that I offer in this book.

Broadly defined, *emotional states* are affective responses to triggering events that activate issues related to both survival and inner well being. These states are mobilized by external (and, more rarely, internal) *triggering events*, and they are experienced both consciously and unconsciously. They have both psychological and physical features, and their physiological, biochemical, and brain substrates have been intensely investigated.

For our purposes, we may classify four types of basic emotional arousal: first, *negative emotional states*, such as fear, anxiety, and rage, which are affects that function as emergency signals and physical and mental mobilizing responses to predatory threat and physical and psychological danger; second, *positive emotional states*, such as love and happiness, which are activated in the service of needs for care, safety, relatedness, and reproductive success; third, *depressive affective states*, *which* are reactions to loss and experienced harm; and, fourth, *moral emotional states*, such as shame and guilt, which serve mainly to limit harmful actions against others—and the possibility of retribution. Each of these emotional states has a unique neurological substrate and set of physiological correlates, much of it centred in the limbic system and its linkages (LeDoux, 1996). In activating and enhancing emergency responses such as withdrawal, flight, or fight, emotions serve the interests of immediate survival and support an individual's use of the adaptive resources needed for coping with acute emotionally charged situations.

The traumas that evoke emotional states may be acute or chronic, physical and/or psychological, and the experiences are both consciously and unconsciously mediated. Clinical study has shown that by and large, acute traumas and the emotional states that they evoke prompt adaptive processing by the *conscious system* of the emotional mind and its superficial unconscious sub-system. Deep unconscious processing is constricted in favour of the mobilization of adaptive resources that are largely accessible to awareness and available for immediate, direct coping responses.

The mental responses to the aftermath of an emotionally charged experience tends to be long-lasting and may persist throughout a lifetime. That is, the disequilibrium and damage caused by traumatic events create lasting mental (and brain) states that often operate dysfunctionally. It is therefore common to find individuals actively engaged in efforts to process and resolve a variety of post-traumatic states and their residuals, however mild or severe. In contrast to moments of sudden emotional charge, this long-term psychological processing effort takes place to only a limited extent consciously but is quite intense on the deep unconscious level. Thus, the conscious processing of the effects of an emotionally charged event tends to be constricted, limited, highly defensive, and perseverative, while the deep unconscious response is likely to be extensive, multifaceted, insightful, and constructive—though unavailable to awareness and to direct adaptive responsiveness.

We may think, then, of an *emotion-producing* mental module (a group of functions related to the development of acute emotional states) and a rather different *emotion-processing* mental module (a group of functions devoted to coping with the after-effects of an emotional state and the trauma or acute need that evoked the emotional response in the first place). Each module is composed of a distinctive set of adaptive functions and each has its own features and processing resources.

In psychotherapy, we are only rarely faced with a patient in the throes of an acute emotional reaction or state. This occurs most often when a patient enters a session in a condition of acute emotional upset such as an anxiety attack, or when a patient is acutely traumatized by his or her therapist. On the other hand, every patient seen in psychotherapy or counselling is actively engaged in processing a host of emotional traumas, as well as moments of joy and a variety of other strong and weak emotionally laden events and impingements.

As we shall see, one group of relatively unappreciated emotionally charged events that lead to extended adaptive processing efforts, especially on the deep unconscious level, pertains to the status of frames and the framing efforts made by others and oneself. Indeed, with respect to emotionally charged experiences, frame-related events are amongst those with the strongest unconscious effects—and they are extremely common occurrences in psychotherapy. In the absence of resolution, the processing of such framing incidents extends for long periods of time. Indeed, adaptive efforts of this kind are central to the psychotherapy experience.

Further implications for psychotherapy

The basic importance throughout nature of frames and framing activities has many implications for psychotherapy. Nature's use of frames offers an avenue through which we can develop invaluable perspectives on the theoretical and practical issues that pertain to the framing of the treatment situation—its setting, ground rules, and boundaries.

Clinical observations clearly indicate that patients and therapists, as part of the vast panorama of nature, very much conform to the general patterns of framing and frame influence. Humans honour the dictum, seen throughout nature, that frames, boundaries, and containers are more fundamental than their contents or contained elements, and they do so with a degree of complexity and impact not seen in lower-level, non-language organisms and systems. It follows, then, that the *contents* of a patient's material in a therapy session are seldom more critical to the dynamic processes and effects of a therapy session than *the status of its frame.*

The most compelling *unconscious* meanings of patients' material are, as a rule, evoked by the currently active frame-related interventions of their therapists. Events outside of therapy and other attributes of therapists' interventions play only a minor role with respect to coping efforts that transpire outside of awareness. Thus, the impact on patients of the verbal contents of therapists' interventions is, in general, far less intense than that caused by their management of the ground rules of therapy—behavioural efforts that speak volumes.

This point makes considerable sense when it is understood that, for example, an assaultive or seductive comment is inherently frame-modifying in that it violates the ground rule calling for a therapist's neutrality. Frame-related attributes critically contextualize and define patients' unconsciously experienced perceptions of therapists' verbalized comments—interpretative and otherwise.

Studies of deep unconscious experience and processing speak against the prevailing idea that rules, boundaries, contexts, and frames are of lesser importance to emotional life and psychotherapy than the intrapsychic and interpersonal events, conflicts, memories, and fantasies experienced and expressed by patients. This is not, however, to argue that the contents of sessions—the feelings, spoken words, and actions of both patient and therapist—are without substantial import for the emotional life of the patient (and therapist) and for the course and outcome of a psychotherapy. The dilemma is resolved by realizing that *the contents and transactions of a psychotherapy session cannot be separated from the status of its frame and the framing activities of the patient and/or therapist*. Indeed, for patients, these very contents and psychodynamics are aspects of their deep unconscious adaptive responses to their therapists' interventions—on this influential level of human experience, contents and framing activities are intertwined. Thus, contents and frame comprise a total gestalt, an amalgam and emergent whole with properties beyond those that either element possesses individually.

At every moment in a treatment experience, implicitly and explicitly, therapists are holding steady, changing, or otherwise managing the ground rules and boundaries of the therapeutic interaction. Handling the ground rules of therapy is a continuous activity of a therapist, even when a particular rule is neglected or goes unenforced. Verbally, a therapist is either intervening or being silent about the ground rules, a choice that is always of great significance. The possibilities range from failing to offer a frame-related intervention when it is called for, to commenting about a ground rule when no intervention is needed, to managing the frame either soundly or improperly. *Dealing with the framework of therapy always uniquely entails both verbalized and behavioural interventions—ultimately both interpretation and management.*

Patients also are continuously active in this area. They are either conforming or not conforming to the frame offered by a therapist—for example, agreeing to a proposed fee or asking for a lesser fee, or being on time or late for their sessions. They may also propose a frame change, which will be in the direction of either modifying or securing a particular ground rule. The therapist is then obligated eventually to respond in some fashion—a response that should, as we shall see, be based mainly on the patient's accompanying encoded, unconscious directives. •

At all times, then, frame-related activities are a primary concern of and issue for all patients and therapists. Clinical studies indicate that quite universally *the deep unconscious level of experience*, as conveyed by patients' encoded communications in a psychotherapy session, is primarily organized around, evoked by, and reflective of patients' attempts to adapt unconsciously to the framing activities of their psychotherapists—and secondarily to their own frame-related actions should they occur. Such is the adaptation-evoking power of frame-related transactions.

The observational base

Many of these statement about frames and framing are unfamiliar to practising psychotherapists. We must therefore address the observational basis for these ideas, the means of listening and formulating patients' material that accounts for these precepts. Indeed, the mode of listening comes first and is most fundamental; propositions about framing interventions and the ground rules unfold from this essential base.

By and large, the ideas presented here are derived from clinical studies based on *the communicative approach to psychotherapy and psychoanalysis*. This approach stresses the role of *unconscious perception and deep unconscious processing activities* in all aspects of emotional life and adaptation, and insists clinically on *unconscious or encoded substantiation as a test of an intervention's validity*. The result is frame-related thinking and clinical precepts that share some features with, yet depart significantly from, mainstream analytic and non-analytic thinking about the ground rules of psychotherapy (e.g. see Bollas & Sundelson, 1996; Gabbard & Lester, 1995).

The divergences in these two viewpoints stem largely from the means by which present-day therapists, as compared to communicative therapists, observe and formulate the material from patients. Non-communicative therapists and counsellors base their frame-related thinking and practices on readings of patients' *manifest contents and consciously fashioned communications*. The unconscious aspects of these formulations, if they are at all developed, tend to be self-evident: they involve purported genetic connections and *inference-making*—the formulation of a type of latent content that entails identifying unrecognized implications of, and patterns reflected in, the surface of messages.'

As we shall see, this level of communication reflects the operations of the *conscious system* of the *emotion-processing mind*—the mental module with which humans adapt to emotionally charged triggering events and their meanings. The focus in this work is, then, on the boundary or container of human communication without sufficient consideration of the contents and messages that lie within that container, especially those that are encoded. This effort is not unlike looking at the edges of a river but missing all of the centre-stream activity.

' In contrast, the listening and formulating of the communicative approach encompasses not only the implications of these manifest contents, but also draws on a set of deeper unconscious, disguised meanings.' These camouflaged latent contents are adaptive responses to emotionally charged triggering events and involve *encoded themes* that are conveyed in the narrative images of patients' communications to their therapists. This level of expression reflects the operations of the second system of the emotion-processing mind—*the deep unconscious system*—which is an enormous adaptive resource.

Patients' emotional adaptations and communicative expressions are, on the *deep unconscious level*, primarily constituted as responses to emotionally charged, immediate triggering events or *environmental impingements*—a term that encompasses *stimuli derived from both living and non-living surroundings, contexts, communications, and activities*. For humans, environments have both physical and psychological features. In psychotherapy and counselling, impingements that pertain to the setting, boundaries, and ground rules—the framework—of a therapy are especially powerful. Thus, the therapist's management of the frame is critical to a patient's therapeutic experience and to his or her possibilities for a deeply insightful, adaptive cure.

Considerable confusion about the validity of the precept of the centrality of the ground rules of psychotherapy and of therapists' frame-related interventions arises because the two systems of the emotion-processing mind—conscious and deep unconscious—operate quite independently of each other. Fatefully, they also have evolved very different needs, attitudes, and behavioural preferences as they pertain to the ground rules of therapy. In essence, the conscious system is frame-insensitive and generally inclined towards frame modifications, whereas the deep unconscious system is exceedingly frame-sensitive and consistently inclined towards secured frames.

The level of basic listening adopted by a therapist or counsellor, be it manifest and conscious-system–oriented or latent/encoded and deep-unconscious-system–oriented, will profoundly influence his or her understanding of the role of the frame and framing interventions in the psychotherapeutic process. It is impossible to reach across the chasm that separates the two systems of the emotion-processing mind so as to sustain a position that embraces the contradictory positions of its conscious and deep unconscious systems. Nevertheless, inevitably, every therapist must make a choice as to which system's dictates he or she will use as a guide to therapeutic practice.

Further perspectives

Strange indeed is the realization that sensitivity to the inordinately powerful effects of rules, frames, and boundaries has been relegated to a deeply unconscious rather than conscious system of the human mind. As we shall see, this aspect of the evolved architecture of the emotion-processing mind has arisen largely in response to language acquisition and the emergence of existential death anxiety (see chapter six; see also Langs, 1996).

Among the additional practical consequences of this mental design feature, *trigger decoding* the themes in patients' narratives—deciphering their disguised meanings in light of their evocative stimuli—is the only currently available means of accessing and fathoming deep unconscious experience. Because therapists' frame-related interventions are the main triggers to which this deep unconscious system is most responsive, it is, then, solely by this means that a therapist—and patient—can appreciate the extensive ramifications and influence of framing efforts and the framework of psychotherapy.

This situation arises because the frame-related adaptations of the deep unconscious system are guided by a set of needs and preferences that sharply differ from the adaptive responses of the conscious system. In addition, deep unconscious frame preferences are far more constructive and health-giving than those of the conscious system. Furthermore, deep unconscious experience outweighs conscious experience as a motivating factor and force in emotional life and in the outcome of a psychotherapy. Throughout this book, I therefore pay particular attention to the reliable and consistent encoded adaptive responses of patients to their therapists' frame-related interventions.

Deep unconscious responses as reflected in encoded derivatives speak against the prevailing idea that unless critically damaged or impaired, the ground rules or framework of a psychotherapy recedes into the background of the therapeutic interaction and experience. Nor are the ground rules of therapy entirely fixed entities. The framework of a therapy is relatively set in some respects yet quite fluid in others. Furthermore, every moment of holding a frame secured or actively modifying it, no matter how seemingly minor, is of great significance for both members of the therapeutic dyad.

There is, in all, a broad agreement that a secured framework of a psychotherapy creates a background of safety and a holding environment for a therapy patient, but the definition and properties of a secured frame have eluded a clear consensus. In addition, there is a far less extensive sense that a modified frame is harmful to patients. However, the communicative approach proposes three major caveats to these ill-defined ideas: first, that the realm of ground rules and frames actually touches on both the prevailing conditions of a treatment experience and the framing activities of therapists and, at times, their patients; second, that these conditions and activities are central to the deep unconscious experience of therapy patients (and their therapists); and third, that frame-related experiences are encoded in the evoked narrative-images contained in patients' communications in sessions.

For patients in psychotherapy, on the deep unconscious level of experience, framing activities are both figure and ground. They are the contexts and conditions for working though disruptive interpersonal and intrapsychic conflicts, and they are also the most immediate and compelling activators of these symptomatic issues. *In substance, at the deep unconscious level, the curative aspects of psychotherapy are centered primarily around the negotiation of framing activities by both patients and therapists.*

The Freudian position places unconscious fantasies, especially those that are oedipal, murderous of the father, and incestuous, as the fundamental source of "neuroses" (Hogenson, 1983). Freudian therapy is therefore focused on eliciting direct or disguised versions of these fantasies in the context of the interaction with the analyst. This model stresses the projection of genetically driven, internal contents onto the therapist and directs the therapist away from external reality and the immediate therapeutic environment, and therefore away from the framework or conditions of psychotherapy.

Latter-day relational theorists have modified this position by viewing interpersonal conflict as the main source of human maladaptations (Langs, 1988). However, these writers formulate relationships and interactions in broad, ill-defined terms and they fail to examine in detail the specific implications of therapists' interventions. Furthermore, they lack a strong, definitive, moment-to-moment adaptational approach and they do not engage in trigger decoding. As a result, they pay little or no attention to the framework of therapy and see the inner experiences of reality impingements as constructions made by the mind of the patient or by the minds of the patient and therapist conjointly. These therapists tend to overlook the consensually validated, universal properties of external events and do not examine how these attributes impact on and constrain patients' internally coloured interpretations. All in all, relational therapists retain the Freudian focus on patients' inner minds and fail to take into account the specific adaptation-evoking, environmental triggering events with which patients are faced from moment-to-moment within and outside of their psychotherapies.

In contrast, the communicative approach is based on a strong adaptational position that sees adaptations to specific environmental events, particularly those that are immediate or recent, as the primary function of all organisms, including patients in psychotherapy. The approach affords conscious and especially unconscious *perception* primacy over conscious and unconscious *fantasy*. It also stresses the importance of *deep unconscious adaptive responsiveness to environmental impingements*. In this context, the condition-setting framework of therapy and the framing interventions of therapists take on great importance. Furthermore, the usual stress on individual responsiveness is supplemented by a full appreciation of the universal adaptive resources of patients that are constituted through the basic architecture of the emotion-processing mind.

* * *

Every living being is framed by its environment and is defined in its interactions as a system comprised of self and other. Conceptualizing psychotherapy in terms of *the patient–therapist system* is another approach that brings framing to the fore. All systems have boundaries and operate according to rules, and both of these aspects are vital to the system's functioning and survival. These principles inevitably must apply to the patient–therapist system as it operates in the therapy situation.

Of special import for living entities, and for humans in particular, is the relatively neglected psychophysical boundary between life and death. The *existential rule of life* is that life is surrounded at both ends by non-existence, and it makes especially clear that death follows life. This fundamental rule of human existence casts a shadow across all human reactions to rules, frames, and boundaries. It is a basic canon that evokes significant degrees of conscious and especially deep unconscious death anxiety. Because these anxieties are frame-related, they affect patients' and therapists' attitudes and behaviours towards all aspects of frames and framing (Langs, 1997). This, too, will concern us as this book unfolds.

The essential thesis of this book

As you may have surmised, the main thesis of this book is that the status and management of the ground rules, setting, frames, and boundaries of psychotherapy and counselling are critical and deeply affecting adaptive issues for both patients and therapists. While the conscious experiences of both parties to therapy tend only intermittently to attend to frame impingements, their deep unconscious minds are at all times intensely concentrated on and affected by this area of activity and meaning.

Almost all of the psychodynamic and conflictual issues that patients work over *deeply unconsciously* in therapy are evoked by framing events, as are their activated genetic connections, behavioural consequences, and other conscious and unconscious implications. It is these deep unconscious efforts at adaptation and processing that most powerfully influence the vicissitudes of a psychotherapy experience and determine its outcome.

Because of the basic design of the emotion-processing mind, therapists' framing activities—handling and interpreting ground-rule issues and impingements—are their most important therapeutic task and securing frames their most healing intervention. Successful negotiation of this aspect of treatment requires that therapists develop deep insights into their own frame related-attitudes, preferences, and actions.

There are many sources of resistances to achieving this goal. Some, like the dread of secured frames because of the existential death anxieties that they evoke, are universal and inherent to the evolved design of the emotion-processing mind. Some are social and professional because modified frames are advocated by health-management organizations and professional colleagues, as is the defensive denial of the harmful effects of these modifications. And some are personal in terms of a therapist's life history. In this respect, experiences with trauma—incidents that almost always involve frame violations—are quite important, as is the extent to which his or her parents secured and maintained aspects of the framework of the nuclear family situation and the degree to which they violated frames themselves and selectively sanctioned particular frame modifications in their offspring. Finally, there are the frame-related experiences that arise in a therapist's own personal psychotherapy—much of it frame-deviant in today's climate of practice. The pursuit of emotional truths pertaining to the ground rules and frames of psychotherapy is an arduous, yet exceedingly rewarding, task for all psychotherapists.

A historical perspective

Freud's genius led him to devote about half of his fundamental papers on the technique of psychoanalysis to its ground rules (Freud, 1912, 1913; Langs, 1976). His main point was that these rules safeguard the patient's so-called transferences and the analytic work by allowing the treatment to unfold in terms of the patient's rather than the therapist's emotional needs and neurosis. Implicit in his thinking is the idea that modifications in the ground rules of psychoanalysis and psychotherapy are expressions of analysts' countertransferences, a point that he did not, however, develop to any appreciable extent.

As is often the case with psychotherapists, Freud's recorded precepts were at variance with his actual behaviour. He used a home-office; shared his office with his daughter Anna, whom he analysed; was prone to extensive personal self-revelations to his patients; analysed colleagues and their wives and mistresses; discussed his analytic work with friends and with relatives of his patients, including colleagues who referred their lovers to him; and openly sanctioned an enormous number of blatant frame deviations—sexual liaisons among them—by his colleagues, students, and analysands (Gabbard & Lester, 1995).

Of the many implications of these historical facts, two are especially pertinent for our pursuits. First, these frame-modifying inclinations, which were the rule among the first generation of psychoanalysts, reflect the in-built, natural tendency of the conscious mind/system to prefer frame modifications to secured frames. This suggests that therapists are unlikely to engage in sound frame-managing efforts unless they self-process and overcome the universal conscious tendency to deviate—an inclination that is a product of both the architecture of the emotion-processing mind and personal psychodynamic factors.

Second, the deviant-frame activities of the early analysts created a heritage that supported similar tendencies in their analysands, which were then passed down through generations of psychotherapists. This legacy involves both conscious and unconscious messages and is supported by defensively designed, non-validated theoretical constructs and pathological unconscious identificatory processes. Accepting a more sage and valid view of framing will require that psychotherapists overcome their professional legacies along with other sources of resistance.

The goals of the book

With these perspectives in mind, I now list the main goals and intentions of this book.

1. To offer an extensive exploration of the nature, functions, and effects of the ground rules of psychotherapy as they are created, sustained, and modified by both therapists and their patients.

2. To base this exploration on a clinical listening and formulating

process of patients' communications that takes into account both manifest meanings and implications, as well as latent, encoded meanings.

3. To offer extensive evidence that therapists' framing efforts constitute the most critical adaptation-evoking group of triggers for patients' deep unconscious experiences within the treatment situation.

4. To demonstrate that the status of the framework of a psychotherapy, and its management and interpretation by the therapist, are the most powerful determinants unconsciously of the vicissitudes of a patient's symptoms and the overall outcome of his or her psychotherapy.

5. To define the ideal set of ground rules for a therapeutic experience and to examine each component ground rule in detail—its configuration, meanings, management, and interpretation.

6. To identify the set of *universal meanings* that accrue to frames of psychotherapy that are ideally set and to those that are compromised in any way.

    a. To complement this understanding of core features with an appreciation for the *individual differences and personal sensitivities* that prompt patients to respond selectively to the universal meanings of frames and framing activities.

    b. To account comprehensively for both the inherent nature of reality and the subjective construction of the meanings of reality events as constrained by the particular features of each environmental impingement.

7. To examine the polarities that delineate two relatively distinct universes of psychotherapy defined by the status of its ground rules—*secured-frame and deviant-frame modes of treatment.*

8. To identify the key factors in the framing attitudes and behaviours of both patients and therapists. In this regard, the particular effects of the evolved design of the emotion-processing mind and of the fact of human mortality are afforded special attention here. The much-neglected relationship between death anxiety and the framing of psychotherapy is explored and clarified in some detail.

9. To integrate and extend my considerable but scattered writings on rules, frames, and boundaries, synthesizing these ideas into a comprehensive viewpoint (Langs, 1976, 1979, 1982, 1992, 1993, 1995).

10. To offer a set of sound, *unconsciously validated* clinical precepts related to how therapists can best establish, manage, and interpret the ground rules and setting of a psychotherapy in ways that best serve the interests of their patients—and themselves.

11. To offer a thorough investigation of the ground rules of clinic and other non-private forms of psychotherapy.* The particular nature of psychotherapy conducted in these settings, and the unique problems of technique that they pose, will receive considerable attention.

12. Finally, to describe the particular nature of a therapeutic experience that unfolds within an entirely private and secured therapy setting and to examine the special problems that are likely to arise under such conditions.

This is a large and compelling agenda. Let us turn now to the task of fulfilling its many challenging features.

---

*For ease of presentation, throughout the book I use the term *clinic* to allude to the wide range of treatment settings that exist outside a therapist's private office. These include offices in health-maintenance organizations and other types of health-care plans, hospitals, employee health centres, work with patients in their homes or while they are hospitalized, and a host of other public and semi-private settings.

CHAPTER TWO

Frames and conscious and unconscious experience

T he results of investigations into psychotherapy depend on the conceptual framework within which they are carried out and the consequent selection of methods of study. Beginning with Freud (1912, 1913), a moderate literature on rules, frames, and boundaries has developed based essentially on observations and formulations that pertain to a patient's overt behaviours and manifest communications, and their evident but latent implications (Langs, 1976).

The more recent literature on this subject has been motivated primarily by a heightened awareness of the detrimental consequences of therapists' *gross* frame violations, such as sexual seduction of patients (Gabbard & Lester, 1995) and by the growing number of modifications of the total privacy and confidentiality of therapies that take place in settings that involve third-party payers and ancillary personnel (Bollas & Sundelson, 1996). However, because the ideas offered in such writings are based on direct communications from patients, there is debate over the extent to which these actions and conditions of therapy disturb the treatment process and harm patients. Therapists have developed many arguments that serve to deny the detrimental effects of blatant frame modifications, even though there is a growing sense that maintaining ground rules in these areas is the safest course that a therapist can take.

As I have indicated, these approaches to understanding frames and framing rely on conscious experiences and communication. They tap into *conscious system* assessments that are highly defensive, insensitive to many nuances of framing and its effects, and unconsciously self-defeating and self-punitive. In addition, these surface-oriented clinical studies fail to define fully the salutary effects of secured frames. They also entirely miss the existence of secured-frame anxieties—the unconscious conflicts and issues caused by sound adherence to the ideal ground rules of therapy. The links between death anxiety and frames go unrecognized in this work.

To clarify further the differences and agreements between the classical analytic and communicative views of the ground rules of psychotherapy and counselling, let us now examine more closely the nature of conscious experience and deep unconscious experience as these pertain to frames and framing.

Listening and the view of the mind

As I have been emphasizing, non-communicative listening and formulating focuses on surface contents and their purported implications and unconscious links with the past. This approach leads to a *single-system view* of the emotion-processing mind as a relatively integrated entity with conscious, preconscious, and unconscious components, and censorships or defensive barriers of repression between each component. The unconscious part of the mind is seen mainly as a *receptacle* for forbidden meanings, and the primary sources of conflict and repression are said to lie with inner instinctual-drive wishes and fantasies.

In this scheme, external reality may activate these inner wishes, but, on the whole, reality stands as a secondary emotional factor. In an effort to afford the outer world—and especially relationships with others—a more compelling role in understanding emotional dysfunctions, interpersonal and relational theorists have shifted their focus on the etiology of emotional maladaptations to interactions with others. In their view, which is also based on *manifest-content listening*, inputs from significant others activate conflicts and need-systems from which patients may benefit or suffer—ultimately, however, the main issues lie within the inner mental world of the patient.

In contrast, communicative listening and formulating attends to surface contexts, but relies mainly on *trigger decoding* patients' narrative material and studies both perceptions and inner responses. On this basis, the thesis of a *two-system emotion-processing mind* was proposed and clinically verified (Langs, 1995, 1996). The first system is termed *the conscious system* because its perceptions, fantasies, and adaptive efforts are accessible to awareness and are reflected in overt behaviours. This system is our basic long- and short-term survival system, and it therefore needs to operate on the basis of direct experience and surface meanings, to the relative exclusion of those that are encoded or symbolized—dealing with real dangers and the search for safety are its prime adaptive tasks.

The unconscious component of this system is called *the superficial unconscious subsystem of the conscious system*. It is a subsystem that embodies and processes events whose relatively evident but painful meanings are blocked from awareness—that is, subjected to *superficial unconscious repression*. These meanings prove to be retrievable in forms that are either thinly disguised or manifestly stated. This is seen, for example, when a therapist has been late in beginning a session and the patient tells a story about a mother who served dinner late one night—the narrative minimally disguises the therapist's lateness.

The second fundamental system of the emotion-processing mind is called *the deep unconscious system*. It operates on the basis of incoming information and meanings that are *unconsciously rather than consciously perceived* and are then processed by a *deep unconscious wisdom subsystem*. The deep unconscious system has its own ego, superego, and id functions and capabilities, and it operates on the basis of premises and needs that are strikingly different from those embraced by the conscious system—especially with respect to rules, frames, and boundaries.

Both the unconscious perceptions of environmental events and the results of their deep unconscious processing are barred entry into direct awareness. That is, *the conscious mind has no undisguised access to deep unconscious experience*. Even though deep unconscious processing efforts are far more insightful and constructive than conscious processing, deep unconscious perceptions and adaptive processing efforts are *represented in awareness only in encoded form via the displaced and disguised narratives themes* communicated by patients in the course of free associating.

To ascertain the nature of deep unconscious experiences, then, it is necessary to *trigger decode* the patients' narrative themes. This is carried out by using the adaptation-evoking triggering event (e.g. an increase in the fee for sessions) as the decoding key with which to organize and unravel the patient's unconscious perceptions and experienced meanings that are encoded (disguised) in the patient's narrative images (e.g. a story of a greedy, selfish spouse). As noted, for psychotherapy patients, the most compelling triggers as they pertain to deep unconscious experience are the frame-related interventions of their therapists.

Comparing the two modes of experience

The perceptions and experiences of the conscious system tend to be relatively frame-insensitive. The conscious mind is far more focused on survival issues and psychodynamic meanings than on frames. Conscious experience is concerned with a wide array of environmental impingements, among which ground-rule transactions are, in general, of minor import. Furthermore, the conscious system tends to favour frame-modifying over frame-securing actions.

In contrast, unconscious perceptions and deep unconscious experience are almost entirely focused on frame-related transactions and their meanings, and encoded communication consistently speaks for secured rather than modified frames. The concentration of deep unconscious system experience on frames and framing efforts, and conscious system experience on a broad range of activities, issues, and circumstances with little attention afforded to

frame impingements, is one of the most crucial differences between these two systems of the mind. As a result, the conscious
mind has difficulty grasping and appreciating the nature and importance of deep unconscious experience and an individual's basic
frame-related needs and attitudes.

The differences between these two modes of emotional experience explain why a patient's or therapist's understanding of the
effects of the ground rules of psychotherapy are very different
on the conscious and deep unconscious levels, and indicate why
their appreciation of the role of the framework of therapy depends
on the level of experience on which they base their assessments.
Because the value systems of the two systems of the emotion-
processing mind are so different, conscious evaluations of the
ground rules differ considerably from those made deeply unconsciously. But even more fundamentally, conscious and deeply
unconscious frame-related needs and adaptive preferences are at
opposite poles. As a result, *conscious system psychotherapy* is a mode
of therapy that is strikingly different from *deep unconscious system
psychotherapy*, especially with respect to framing and managing
the frame of a therapy experience. In general, mainstream forms of
therapy and counselling are likely to be framed in much looser
and deviant fashion than communicative forms of psychotherapy.

A clinical excerpt may help to clarify this discussion. Ms
Shaw,* a depressed woman in her early 30s, was in psychotherapy with Dr Clark, a male therapist. One year into her
therapy, the patient began a session by indicating that she had
to be out of town on business the following week. She was
therefore cancelling her hour and reminded Dr Clark that she
had been told that she was allowed to do so as long as she gave
24-hour notice. Dr Clark responded by pointing out that the
ground rules also called for a make-up session if at all possible.
He looked into his appointment book and suggested a time for

---

*The vignettes offered in this book are fictitious. However, they faithfully
reflect clinical experience, and the reader can compare these generic examples
with his or her own clinical experience. These excerpts are offered solely to
illustrate and give narrative form to the main points of the book.

an additional session during the week following the pending absence. Ms Shaw agreed to be at that session, and she expressed her appreciation that her therapist could accommodate her as he had. Her parents had seldom responded to her needs when she was a child.

After a pause, Ms Shaw said that she was thinking of an incident that had occurred during the previous weekend. She hadn't realized how upsetting it had been. She had made a date for Friday night with her boyfriend, Ted, but he kept calling her to change their plans. He was ridiculously controlling and unpredictable; it was annoying and crazy-making—he should be more consistent.

When they finally got together, they went back to her apartment and he wanted to pay for a bed she had recently purchased. She rejected his offer because it seemed like he was trying to make her into a prostitute. She also didn't want to be obligated or enslaved to him. Despite her entreaties, he seemed unable to understand that it was her bed and the cost should be her responsibility. On top of that, he insisted on going to bed with her and having sex even though she was exhausted and wanted to wait until morning. He got his way, but she felt manipulated and furious with him, that it was no way to treat someone you love. Was she right about all of this, or was she being insensitive? Ted's father had died recently, and he had been having a difficult time getting over the loss.

This is an example of a common, loosely structured approach to the ground rules of psychotherapy. In many situations, the ground rules are not articulated at all, except for the fee and perhaps the time of the sessions. The other aspects of the frame are then established—if at all—as the therapy moves along, or the ground rules may be vaguely defined, left uncertain, and handled flexibly as frame issues arise. Only rarely are most or all of the ground rules specifically delineated in the consultation session, as they should be. In all, the prevailing credo has been one of flexibility, tact, and common sense—within uncertain limits, unevenly applied (Gabbard & Lester, 1995).

Having described a general approach to specifying the ground rules of a psychotherapy, note should be made that these trends are being challenged by many managed-care companies and state legislatures—among others. Operating in terms of conscious experience, though often in defiance of conscious sensibilities, these agencies have been dictating policies such as full written disclosure of such frame-related matters as the fee structure, session-cancellation policies, rights to records, the introduction of second therapists and their opinions into a treatment situation, confidentiality, goals of treatment, and more. This insistence on patently insecure and deviant frames does considerable damage to patients, therapists, and the therapeutic process on both the conscious and deep unconscious levels of experience—effects that are usually overlooked or denied by all concerned.

Returning to the clinical example, we may note that it touches on the ground rule pertaining to the time and day of a patient's sessions. The rule that Dr Clark had adopted held his patient responsible for her sessions unless she notified him of a cancellation at least twenty-four hours beforehand. Dr Clark also had established an option, depending on his schedule, that allowed him to offer the patient a make-up hour, which the patient was obliged to accept and pay for if she could be available for the session.

In general, this kind of loose, open-to-judgement statement of an aspect of the ground rules of psychotherapy is acceptable to the conscious mind, but not to deep unconscious experience. The conscious mind agrees to and even seeks all kinds of poorly defined ground rules and often argues for the flexible maintenance of, and exceptions to, these basic tenets. However, the deep unconscious system supports and validates through encoded themes only those ground rules that are strictly and properly defined and sustained, and it does so in light of both evolutionary (adaptive) wisdom and personal deep unconscious experiences of frames and framing efforts by parents and others, from infancy on.

This difference between the frame attitudes of the two systems of the emotion-processing mind is aligned with another contrast in positions: the conscious experience of frames and ground rules varies enormously from person to person, be they a patient or a therapist, while deep unconscious experience is strikingly consistent across individuals and over time in these respects—*encoded images always speak for securing and sustaining the ideal ground rules of therapy*. Individual differences are embedded within this collective tendency and are reflected in the selection for response of particular unconsciously experienced meanings of a therapist's frame-related intervention from its universal attributes. The consistency of deep unconscious frame-related experiences and assessments, and the existence of architecturally created universal proclivities, are sources of confusion and alienation for conscious minds because this part of the mental apparatus is so varied in its approaches to these same areas. The conscious mind is also disturbed by deep unconscious thinking and inclinations regarding the framework and ground rules because they differ so much from its own tendencies.

In the vignette, Dr Clark offered a make-up session immediately after Ms Shaw cancelled her hour. Technically, before responding in substance to the patient's announcement, he should have directed her to continue to say whatever came to mind. On that basis, he could have defined the patient's conscious and unconscious responses to the anticipation that he would not be holding her responsible for the fee for the cancelled session and her expectation that a make-up hour would be proposed. This approach would facilitate the patient's expression of narratives that inevitably would encode her deep unconscious perceptions of these *anticipated frame modifications*. A therapist's immediate manifest response to a patient's frame-related proposal tends to confine the exchange to unencoded manifest contents, and to conscious system experience and values, thereby precluding expressions of the invaluable adaptive wisdom of the deep unconscious part of the mind. Such work also severely limits the therapist's range of understanding of the meanings and consequences of framing efforts.

Therapists who listen and formulate on the basis of direct associations and their meanings are inclined to act quickly in response to ground-rule problems, believing that they should be disposed of so that the patient can get back to his or her "real issues". They fail to realize that on the deep unconscious level of experience, these "real issues" are activated and brought to life by these very same frame-management interventions, nor do they understand that these seeming trivialities by conscious standards are compelling adaptation-evoking triggers fraught with real and extensive consequences by deep unconscious standards.

By waiting for his patient's narrative material, Dr Clark would have the great advantage of eventually being in a position to trigger decode his patient's deep unconscious responses to these anticipated triggering events. This would be done by linking the encoded themes to the expected frame-related interventions of the therapist—here, the foregoing of the fee for the cancelled hour and the offer of a make-up session (both are frame-deviant). In so doing, the themes are treated as the patient's personally selected, valid, deep unconscious perceptions and adaptation-promoting assessments of the therapist's anticipated frame-related proposals. The encoded images will most certainly speak for adhering to the uncompromised ground rule of holding the patient responsible for the fee for all scheduled sessions and for not offering a make-up hour at another time—adhering to the ground rule of a set time and day for the sessions.

In the session at hand, the therapist intervened immediately, accepted the patient's proposed frame modification, and then created an additional frame-deviant trigger—the offer of the make-up session. These departures from the ideal frame are emotionally charged triggering events to which the patient was then compelled to adapt. She responded to these triggers *consciously* with manifest appreciation for the therapist's generosity and flexibility. But she then shifted to the narrative mode—to encoded communication—and generated a story that conveyed, through the use of displacement and disguise, her *deep unconscious* assessment and adaptive reactions to these same triggering events.

How, then, does her story about her boyfriend decode in response to the two frame-deviant triggering events that we have identified—foregoing the fee for a scheduled session and offering a make-up hour?

To establish a connection between an encoded narrative and a triggering event, we look first for *themes that bridge from the surface story to the identity or meaning of the trigger that has evoked the encoded themes*. With the bridging or connecting themes identified, we extract the remaining powerful themes in the patient's imagery and transpose them into apposition with the triggering event—that is, we undo the use of displacement. We then formulate these themes as *personally selected, valid unconscious perceptions* of the unconsciously mediated meanings of the frame-related trigger. In addition, because these themes reflect deep unconscious modes of adaptation, we search for *encoded correctives, models of rectification*—directives to the therapist as how best to manage the frame. These two types of encoded communications—*meaning, management*—point to the precept that in the area of ground rules, both interpretation and frame management are required of the therapist.

In the vignette, the first part of Ms Shaw's encoded story contains a *bridging theme* in the allusion to her fiancé's insistence that she take money from him. The theme of money bridges to the fee, and the gift of money derivatively represents through analogy one meaning of the therapist's foregoing his fee for the cancelled session (Haskell, 1991; Langs, 1992): it is a gift of money to the patient. Ms Shaw *consciously* indicated her appreciation for this policy; however, *deeply unconsciously* she saw it as making her into a prostitute and depriving her of her independence and autonomy—as a way of obligating and enslaving her to Dr Clark.

The narrative also offers a model of rectification: in her derivative story, the patient does not want the money. This transposes to the therapy situation as an encoded recommendation that the therapist not give the patient the gift of an uncollected fee—that he should charge her for the scheduled hour.

Next, the allusion to her boyfriend's repeatedly changing their scheduled plans bridges to the change in the time and day of the session. Consciously, this offer from the therapist also suited the patient, but deeply unconsciously it was seen as an erratic decision that rendered the therapist quite unpredictable. It was also deeply unconsciously experienced as an attempt to drive the patient crazy, even though, in sharp contrast, the manifest offer of the make-up session was proposed as a way of curing the patient of her "craziness"—her emotional maladaptations. The encoded model of rectification, to the effect that Ted should be more consistent, speaks for the need for a more reliable—that is, fixed and secured—schedule without changes.

The allusion to forced sex is a theme that bridges to the make-up session, which the therapist insisted on holding. Here, too, the patient's conscious response was placid and accepting, but the deep unconscious reaction was quite otherwise. The patient unconsciously experienced the proposal of a different time for her session as a forced seduction. On the deep unconscious level, all such demands of patients by their therapists are experienced as seductive, assaultive, rapacious, and enslaving. This patient's selection of particular unconscious meanings from the many universal implications of this frame-related trigger touch on valid, unconsciously perceived ramifications that have been personally chosen on the basis of her own life experiences and emotional needs. These deep unconscious perceptions will also negatively affect the patient's subsequent behaviours and symptom picture—unless the deviation is properly interpreted and rectified.

For example, Ms Shaw selectively perceived the seductive and rapacious meanings of Dr Clark's offer of the make-up session on the basis of early life experiences with an uncle who lived with her family when she was a child and molested her on several occasions. Thus, the proposed frame modification repeated in symbolic—but real—form these earlier frame-modifying traumas.

The deep unconscious impact of the proposed frame-changes was seen soon after this session, when Ms Shaw over-reacted and flew into a rage at her boyfriend because he insisted on paying for dinner instead of letting her pick up the bill. Unaware of the anxiety and other disturbing effects that her therapist's deviant-frame interventions and proposals were having on her, Ms Shaw displaced her anger at her therapist onto her boyfriend. This kind of entirely unconscious use of displacement is universal and an endless source of grief for all concerned.

Finally, we may note the allusion to the death of Ted's father. As we shall see, the core issue in virtually all frame-modifying situations is that of activated death anxiety (Langs, 1997). Patients who request changes in their hours and therapists who grant them unconsciously are attempting maladaptively to cope with and defend against a death-related issue of some kind. Denying the inevitability of personal death and the death of others is a major function of a large majority of frame modifications.

Based on many unconsciously conveyed clues, Ms Shaw had offered Dr Clark an interpretation to this effect in wondering whether her boyfriend had behaved badly because of the recent death of his father. Dr Clark had in fact recently lost a sister to cancer, and his use of frame-modifying interventions in his work with patients had escalated considerably. Altering ground rules is a common maladaptive, unconscious attempt to lay claim to being an exception to the existential rule that death follows life.

Conscious and deep unconscious frame attitudes

This vignette demonstrates the very different approaches to the rules, frames, and boundaries of the two major systems of the emotion-processing mind. The conscious experience of framing interventions involves minimizing their importance, a relative insensitivity to frame changes, a failure to appreciate the health-giving features of secured frames, a wide difference in responses from one person to the next, a relative insensitivity to the universal properties of frame impingements, and a preference for frame modifications rather than secured frames. These conscious system attitudes are paradoxical because secured frames are safer and more effectively growth-promoting and healing than deviant frames. Indeed, it can be said that conscious frame preferences tend to be self-harmful and geared far more towards maladaptive defence than insight.

In contrast, the deep unconscious experience of frames and framing efforts involves an appreciation for their importance; cognizance of the universal meanings of frame-related triggers; a consistency in responses across individuals; a personally coloured selection of meanings for impact that is unconsciously chosen from the universal implications of a framing intervention; a preference for secured rather than modified frames; and a sensitivity to the inherently harmful, sexual, and aggressive—instinctualized—ramifications of all frame modifications. Deviant frames are deeply unconsciously experienced as assaultive and murderous, and as seductive, incestuous, and promiscuous. Themes of this kind—so-called *power themes*—abound in patients' narrative responses to frame alterations.

In all, the deep unconscious experience of frame-related triggers is far more intense and far less defended than conscious experience. This arises largely because the deep unconscious system can perceive events and their meanings in veridical fashion, no matter how terrible they may be. This level of experience is barred from entering directly into awareness and registers consciously only after being subjected to disguise and encoding.

With respect to the settings, rules, frames, and boundaries of psychotherapy, then, both patients and therapists are of minds divided. We turn now to a closer look at the overall ground rules of therapy in order better to understand the design features of the emotion-processing mind and to develop a practical sense of the attributes of the unconsciously validated, secured framework that apply to all treatment experiences.

CHAPTER THREE

The basic ground rules of psychotherapy

Although fraught with uncertainty in many quarters, the present-day ground rules of psychotherapy in use by a majority of psychotherapists and counsellors are the result of a process of cultural evolution that has taken place over the past 100 years or so. The need for rules and boundaries was evident to Freud (1912, 1913), even though he was in most respects a frame-deviant psychoanalyst (Gabbard & Lester, 1995). In subsequent years, the problem of defining an optimal set of rules and conditions for psychoanalysis and psychotherapy has defied a clear solution. Therapists still cannot agree on which ground rules are essential to a secure therapy experience, nor is there a consensus as to the latitude or narrowness within which a therapist can properly manage the frame. Adding to the confusion, many therapists claim that there is no such entity as a universal frame or set of ground rules that applies to all patients and therapy situations. They propose instead that each patient requires a framework suited to his or her particular needs and in keeping with a variety of circumstances that have a bearing on the locale and general conditions under which that patient is seen (e.g. Weiss & Sampson, 1986). As we shall see, this proposition, based on conscious system thinking, is untenable by deep unconscious system standards.

These uncertainties as to the definition and functions of the ground rules of therapy stem mainly from manifest content listening and formulating; the absence of a sound validating methodology; the use of the highly variable and unreliable attitudes and values of the conscious system with respect to framing decisions; unexplored personal biases; experiences with personal life events and psychotherapies in which frame modifications have transpired; and failures to pursue carefully and evaluate the consequences of therapists' frame-related interventions.

When trigger decoding is utilized to determine patients' deep unconscious responses to framing interventions, the picture of the ground rules of psychotherapy radically departs from manifest content-based views. Not only are the functions of the frame and the framing efforts of therapists clarified, but we also find that on the deep unconscious level of experience, patients are very consistent in their framing needs and views of therapists' frame-related efforts. Decoding patients' narrative responses to therapists' framing activities and interpretations allows for a sound assessment of these endeavours and an appreciation of their short- and long-term effects on patients. With utmost regularity, patients' deep unconscious responses to framing interventions have shown that at a fundamental psychobiological level, patients and therapists show an unswerving need for secured frames and clear interpersonal boundaries.

The manner in which a therapist addresses and responds to patients' deep unconscious, secured-frame needs is fateful for the vicissitudes of patients' emotional dysfunctions and their therapeutic resolution. The ideal cure takes place within an inherently healing secured frame as supplemented by unconsciously validated interpretations. Under deviant-frame conditions, however, the situation is more complex. Within these frame-altered contexts, relief may be felt by the patient when the damage caused by a frame modification is ignored and, in addition, maladaptive denial-based defences are allowed to flourish and go uninterpreted. Nevertheless, there is a harmful core to these deviant-frame treatment situations, and it takes its toll by unconsciously promoting dysfunctional behaviours and symptoms in patients—disturbances that seldom are linked, as they should be, to the frame-modified therapy conditions.

Another form of relief arises in situations where the frame modifications are inescapable, as when a patient is seen in a clinic setting or privately for a low fee that is necessitated by impoverishment. If the therapist is aware of the frame modifications at hand and continuously interprets their unconscious meanings for the patient using trigger-decoded interventions, many of the harmful effects of these frame deviations can be neutralized. In addition, if the therapist is able to seize the rare opportunity to secure a modified aspect of a basically deviant frame or to hold the frame secured in the face of a patient's attempt or request to deviate, the patient will undergo an enormously healing, *secured-frame interlude*.

It is, then, essential to establish and reach a consensus on the criteria that define the sound and basic ground rules of psychotherapy. Neither a therapist's common sense, conscious preferences, or general knowledge of technique, nor a patient's conscious responses and thoughts about a framing intervention, are suitable for this purpose. Evaluations of ground rules need to be grounded in *unconscious* rather than conscious experience, communication, and validation—the assessments of the deep unconscious system are the only reliable basis for defining the true nature of framing efforts.

The power and wisdom of deep unconscious experience and adaptation are well established (Langs, 1995). It therefore is essential to turn to *trigger decoding and unconscious, encoded validation* as our agreed-upon approach to evaluating the effects of framing interventions and as the means by which we will clarify which ground rules, and in what form, are part of the ideal, optimally healing, *deeply unconsciously sanctioned* framework of psychotherapy.

In clinical practice, this means that whenever a ground rule is established, actively sustained against pressures for change, or modified, the therapist should note the patient's manifest reaction, but should also formulate and take most seriously the patient's latent/encoded responses. Knowledge of these deep unconscious reactions derives entirely from trigger decoding patients' themes and linking them to active frame-related triggers. These themes are organized and interpreted as encoded, valid, deep unconscious perceptions of the actual meanings and implications of the frame-management interventions of the therapist.

To illustrate: Ms Frank asked her therapist, Dr Rand, to reduce his fee because she had become hard-pressed financially. She indicated that she would very much appreciate his doing so.

Dr Rand remained silent and allowed the patient to continue to free associate. Ms Frank went on to add that she needed the fee reduction because she had suffered a recent cutback in her salary. She then shifted to a story about her girlfriend, Beth, who had become a severe alcoholic. Ms Frank blamed her mother for the problem because she had spent her life giving her daughter everything she asked for and indulging her every whim. Recently, when Beth lost her job, her mother stepped right in. Instead of encouraging Beth to find new employment, she gave her a large sum of money. Beth took it and, in little time, had dissipated it on alcohol and drugs. Her mother should have taken a firmer stand; indulging her daughter like that has destroyed both of them—that's what happens when hatred masquerades as love.

The *anticipated frame-related triggering event* here is the possibility or expectation that the therapist will reduce his fee. Consciously, the patient favours the fee reduction and sees it as an act of kindness. The narrative themes, however, encode the patient's valid unconscious perceptions of this frame change as destructively indulgent—as hatred masquerading as love. The *bridging theme* is the offer of money to someone in trouble financially, and the narrative indicates that, deeply unconsciously, the fee reduction would be experienced as a financial sacrifice by the therapist and a gift of money to the patient. The results would be destructive for both parties.

The frame-management advice offered unconsciously to Dr Rand by Ms Frank—*the corrective* or *model of rectification*—is encoded in the story of Beth and her over-indulgent mother. The message is this: the therapist should not indulge the patient with a fee reduction lest it harm both of them. Implied, too, is the suggestion that the therapist should allow the patient to find her way financially, perhaps by getting a better job or finding some other source of additional income.

In the session, Dr Rand made the above interpretation to Ms Frank. She was surprised to realize what she had been communicating. Her next thought was about her friend, Anne, who had lost her job and started her own computer consulting business. She was doing very well now and Ms Frank had the thought that she could do some part time work for Anne to supplement her income.

Next, Ms Frank thought back to an odd situation with her cousin, Millie, whose father was very wealthy. Millie became an artist and her father supported her for a while. But every time Millie took money from him, there was hell to pay. He'd invade her life, start running things, pressure her to get a job, and interfere with her social life. Millie's paintings, which had a lot of promise, began to deteriorate. Finally, in sheer desperation, she refused to see her father and politely told him to keep his money. In little time, she was doing great work again; a gallery took on her paintings and she started to earn a fair amount of money on her own. She did wake up one night and smelled smoke in her apartment, but once her panic that she might be trapped in the apartment had subsided, she was able to find her way to safety. The fire, which was in a stairwell, was extinguished by a neighbour.

Ms Frank paused and suddenly realized the main point of her story. With a laugh, she told Dr Rand to forget the fee reduction: she'd find a way to pay his present fee—and to have a life of her own.

Dr Rand's interpretation and frame-securing efforts obtained encoded validation in the story that Ms Frank told about her cousin Millie—the overly supportive, financially indulgent father (decode as therapist) had been sent away. This was followed by conscious acceptance of these decoded insights. Because conscious endorsement of frame-related interventions is unreliable and varies depending on the status of a patient's secured-frame anxieties and unconscious needs for frame modifications, deep unconscious validation through encoded narratives remains the only reliable means of affirming a frame-related proposal or decision. As reflected in the story of the fire, when the basic frame has been held secure and the frame-management intervention unconsciously validated, these confirming narratives are usually followed by frightening stories about entrapment and/or death. This is a consequence of the *secured-frame, existential death anxieties* that are aroused by validated efforts actively to secure or hold secure the ground rules of a therapy (see chapter five; see also Langs, 1997).

The ideal framework of psychotherapy

The consistency with which the responsive encoded stories from patients' deep unconscious systems validate the need for particular ground rules for psychotherapy is the basis on which we may proceed now to establish *the universal, unconsciously sought for, and validated set of ground rules for an optimal therapeutic experience.*

Many years of study of *the presence or absence of encoded, deep unconscious validation* has revealed that an ideal setting and set of ground rules for all forms of psychotherapy does indeed exist. Despite many disquieting realities that seem to press for departures from this ideal, exceptions to these universal deep unconscious needs for a secured frame are exceedingly rare. Patients with terminal illnesses, for whom existential death anxieties reach an unbearable intensity, may well flee secured-frame therapies, but their encoded themes will nevertheless tend to support the positive features of the ideal frame. In addition, the deep unconscious system often shows an appreciation for the contingencies that, when present, create a compelling need to deviate—for example, seeing a suicidal patient for an extra session (a modification of the ground rule of a set time for all sessions). But here, too, while the frame-modification finds conscious and limited deep unconscious acceptance, strong encoded protests are in evidence. All in all, the *encoded* or *derivative* evidence consistently indicates that departures from these ideals always cause some degree of harm to both patient and therapist.

I now present a well-established set of deeply unconsciously validated ground rules. (For support for this presentation, see Langs, 1979, 1982, 1992, 1993, 1995, 1996. I confine myself here to standard forms of psychotherapy and do not consider the distinctive framework used for the recently developed therapeutic modality, *empowered psychotherapy*: see Langs, 1993.) Some of these tenets may be unfamiliar to the reader, and the entire collection is very likely to be disquieting. Nevertheless, these are unconsciously validated, health-giving ideals, and they are well worth seeking to the fullest extent possible. Deep effects are deep effects, and deep unconscious needs are deep unconscious needs. Frame modifications are harmful, disruptive, pathologically defensive, and costly to all concerned. This clinically validated observation is as inescapable and natural as the discovery that an atmosphere with ample oxygen supports life and one with excess carbon monoxide does not. There is no issue of rigidity here: we are dealing with intrinsic, natural consistencies.

The optimal ground rules of psychotherapy and counselling appear to be the following:

A. *The relatively fixed frame*

1. *The setting*
   - A professional building with a private office and waiting-room, and a toilet in the suite (two, if possible—one for patients, the other for the therapist).
   - A sound-proofed consultation room and, if feasible, a separate exit from the consultation room to the hallway.
   - Modest decor, but no reading materials (their selection is self-revealing).
   - A telephone that is turned off during sessions.
   - A bare desk, chairs, a couch for patients to lie on, no diplomas on the walls, and no bookcases or visible books.
   - Nothing personal or self-revealing in the way of physical objects or mementos.

2. *The time, length, and frequency of sessions*
   - A set day and time for all sessions, including the consultation session. The session is begun and ended strictly as scheduled.
   - A set length for each session, usually forty-five or fifty minutes.
   - A set frequency of sessions, from one to four (ideally one or two) per week.

These ground rules are established in the first (consultation) session, and, ideally, they are not altered for any reason short of a dire emergency or major change in the life circumstances of the patient or therapist. In situations where the choice lies between changing the time and/or day of sessions (and the change must be proposed as a permanent one) or terminating the therapy, the patient's deep unconscious preference, as encoded in his or her material, is likely to be the latter—it is the less deviant of the two possibilities. Thus, the practical decision to make this modification of the frame in order to re-secure it is certain to bring forth from the patient encoded narratives that both validate and invalidate the choice made by the therapist and/or patient because the change has both frame-securing and frame-modifying qualities. ✓

3. *Responsibility for sessions*
   - The patient's commitment to attend and be financially responsible for all scheduled sessions.
   - The therapist's commitment to hold all scheduled sessions except for legal holidays and judicious vacation periods announced at least eight weeks in advance.

4. *Fees*
   - A single, unaltered fee that is commensurate with the therapist's expertise and experience.
   - The acceptance by the patient of full responsibility for paying the fee, which is paid by personal check.
   - Payment made at the beginning of each new month for the prior month's sessions, usually before the start of the first session of the new month.
   - No bill is given to the patient.

B. *The relatively fluid, but firmly held, ground rules*

1. *The absence of censorship*
   - The patient is advised to say whatever comes to mind, without restriction.

2. *The fundamental rule of free association*
   - The patient is advised to let his or her mind wander about without consciously predetermined guidance.

3. *The use of the couch*
   - In dynamic forms of psychotherapy, the couch is recommended because it represents the search for unconscious motives, conflicts, meaning, and experience. For therapists and counsellors who do not have a couch in their office, the face-to-face mode is, in general, an acceptable alternative.

4. *Total privacy and total confidentiality*
   - Except for the referral source, all the transactions that lead up to a consultation session and occur in the course of a psychotherapy are restricted to the patient and therapist exclusively—there are no third parties to the treatment.
   - No notes made by either party to the therapy, whether during or after sessions, and there is no release of information by either party to anyone.
   - There is only one therapist for each patient during a given period of time. While in therapy with a particular therapist, a patient is not to consult with or see another emotional healer. As for the therapist, he or she does not consult with a supervisor, or any other colleague or person, about the therapy.

5. *The relative anonymity of the therapist*
   - The patient and therapist have not had prior contact, professionally or socially.
   - The patient has no knowledge of the therapist's personal life.
   - The referral comes from a professional source or from someone with expertise or knowledge relevant to psycho-

therapy, and is made without the offer of personal information about the therapist.

- Referrals from present or prior patients are not accepted.
- The therapist does not engage in self-revelations of a personal nature, nor does he or she render opinions, advice, or directives.
- There are no revelations about the therapist from third parties.

6. *The use of neutral interventions*
   - The therapist works exclusively with the material available from the patient in each individual session.
   - Interventions are accepted as valid only after they have been confirmed by patients' encoded communications.
   - The use of trigger-decoded interpretations.
   - The exclusion of such interventions as questions, clarifications, and confrontations, because they routinely do not obtain encoded validation.
   - The management of the ground rules towards their securement at the behest of the patient's encoded directives.

C. *Implied ground rules*

1. *The rule of abstinence*
   - Confining the satisfactions of the patient to the experience of a suitable and safe set of conditions for the therapy, the sound management of the ground rules, and the offer of trigger-decoded interpretations that lead to deep unconsciously validated insights.
   - Confining the satisfactions of the therapist to the rewards of properly conducting the psychotherapy and of helping the patient to achieve emotional relief. In addition, the therapist obtains a much-needed source of security in being paid a fee for services rendered.
   - The absence of physical contact.

We must again dispel beliefs or concerns that these ground rules are too rigid, too difficult to establish and maintain, and too problematic for both patients and therapists. The need for a secured frame is a *psycho-biologically based* need and is as immutable as the need for uncontaminated rather than contaminated food. Patients' deep and abiding needs for safe and sound holding and containing do indeed ask a great deal of all concerned. Nevertheless, a therapist's failure to fulfil these needs to the greatest extent possible simply causes serious harm to both parties in the treatment.

As noted earlier, therapists and their patients are unconsciously motivated to find rationalizations to justify their pathological unconscious needs for frame modifications. They are also strongly inclined to deny the hurtful consequences of departures from the ideal frame—when adversity befalls a patient, the role of frame modifications is seldom explored. Nevertheless, both parties to therapy deeply require and benefit from a secured frame; regardless of realistic contingencies, all else is compromised and harmful. The best that can be done under frame-modified conditions is to interpret properly the negative unconscious perceptions and symptomatic effects of the deviations involved and secure those deviations that prove to be unnecessary and correctable. The healing qualities of this understanding and reframing are thereby pitted against the harmful effects of the remaining deviations. This is a difficult battle, but therapists who keep secured all aspects of a frame that can possibly be held secure, and who soundly interpret the patient's experience of the deviant aspects, are likely to be more deeply helpful than harmful.

In this connection, we must address another misconception. The statement of these ideals does *not* imply that psychotherapy cannot be conducted under compromised conditions such as those that exist in clinics and similar settings. It does suggest that deeply insightful therapy must be organized around its frame issues. And it also implies that therapists should strive to keep departures from the ideal frame to an absolute minimum—the field of psychotherapy is plagued by unneeded deviations. As long as a therapist offers the most secured frame possible under the conditions under which a patient is being seen in therapy, viable therapeutic work is feasible. In all, a deep appreciation of the impact of frames and framing interventions renders all forms of psychotherapy far more effective than otherwise.

CHAPTER FOUR

Formulating and intervening with respect to frames

In the course of every psychotherapy session, a patient will unconsciously—and at times, consciously—work over and adapt to the therapist's prevailing frame-related interventions. Even when little attention is paid to these interventions consciously, they are at the core of the patient's *deep unconscious experiences* in therapy. Thus, the patient's encoded narratives will consistently reflect, first, the *nature* of the frame-related intervention with which the patient is coping (i.e. the ground rule that is at issue), and, second, the *personally selected, deep unconscious meanings and impact* that the therapist's framing activities are having on the patient. The component that identifies the ground rule at issue is reflected in *bridging themes* (themes shared by the encoded narrative and the ground rule), while the meaning aspect of the experience is reflected in what are called *power themes* (those of death, illness, harm, and the like—the so-called *damage package*). Power themes arise in response to all frame-related interventions because even though securing the frame evokes positive imagery, both frame-securing and frame-modifying efforts by therapists are endangering for the patient—secured frames evoke existential death anxieties, and modified frames are persecutory.

All of the psychodynamic and interpersonal issues, conflicts, memories, and fantasies that patients work over deeply un- consciously in sessions are activated by their therapists' frame- management and frame-interpretive efforts. Interventions of other types have *little effect on the deep unconscious systems* of the minds of patients in psychotherapy, and they do not obtain deep uncon- scious (encoded) validation. Much the same applies to emotional experiences outside of therapy, in that attempting to interpret their implications without a connection to an active frame issue within the therapy also consistently fails to find deep unconscious confirmation. It can be said again, then, that on the deep uncon- scious level, patients are almost exclusively invested in their thera- pists' framing interventions. An effective psychotherapy needs to be conducted in light of the latter precept.

Perspectives on frame-related listening

Manifest or direct allusions to ground rules by patients are rela- tively infrequent, and, when they do appear, the thinking and preferences that they reflect are quite unreliable. Many ground- rule interventions by therapists go unnoticed consciously, even as they are intensely worked over by the deep unconscious system. While blatant ground-rule deviations may at times draw direct notice and objections from patients, consciously they typically show a preference for frame-deviant interventions that are never- theless harmful to themselves and their therapies. This damage is reflected in patients' encoded images and is actualized through disturbances in their everyday lives and therapies, including seemingly inexplicable negative reactions to their therapists. All in all, direct explorations of frame issues cannot ensure for patients the best possible conditions for their quests for cure, nor can they insightfully modify the deep unconscious basis of their emotional dysfunctions.

Therapeutic work with the framework of a psychotherapy is grounded in an understanding of the encoded derivative messages that framing interventions—interpretive and management—evoke in patients. With respect to a therapist's efforts at comprehension and interpretation, there are two aspects to consider. The first involves *the conscious recognition that a ground-rule intervention has been made*. The second involves *an understanding of the meanings of the patient's encoded responses to these frame-related events*—defining the responsive deep unconscious experience and adaptive recommendations communicated by the patient.

Because of its inherited design and by virtue of psychodynamic factors, the conscious mind is resistant to frame-related realizations in ways that make the recognition of ground-rule impingements a difficult task. While blatant rule changes may readily be noticed if one is alert to this type of transaction (but, even so, may just as easily be missed), moments at which the frame is held secured or modified often elude recognition by both parties to therapy.

Most often, it is the therapist who is impinging on the frame by modifying or securing a particular ground rule. But at times, patients may pressure therapists to alter or secure the frame, or may do so on their own. For example, a patient may ask a therapist for advice (seeking a frame-modifying directive) or brush against the therapist upon entering the consultation room (a frame-modifying physical contact). The therapist may fail to notice his or her own framing efforts, such as beginning a session a minute or two late or extending it by a similar length of time (modifying the agreed-upon length and time of the session) or responding to a patient's question by revealing personal information (a modification of the ground rule of relative anonymity).

Frame impingements, whether frame-securing or frame-modifying, are extremely common in psychotherapy and counselling—and patients are continually adapting to these activities. Therapists need to develop a strong sensitivity to the ground rules of psychotherapy and to the many ways in which the rules can be secured or modified. To illustrate further, easily overlooked are such seemingly minor but significant impingements as patient and therapist going up (or down) the stairs or in an elevator together before or after a session, or their seeing each other on the street or at a concert or in a department store (modifications of the ground rule that contact between them be restricted to the therapist's office), or other obvious frame modifications such as a change in the time of a session or a knock on the consultation-room door by an outsider during a session.

Blatant frame-related events of this kind are *seldom alluded to directly* by patients in their sessions, even when they take place during a session or just before it is to begin. Yet the patient's encoded themes will clearly relate to the frame impingement and indicate that the deep unconscious system has been all the while quite alert to the frame issue, even when it seems innocuous or irrelevant to the conscious mind.

Some technical precepts

As noted, the handling of ground-rule impingements calls for both *interpretation and rectification* (if possible). *This is done entirely in keeping with and at the behest of the patient's encoded communications.*

The clinically validated rules of interpreting require that an interpretive intervention be made by a therapist only when a patient has provided two key elements: *a manifest allusion to the adaptation-evoking, frame-related triggering event*, and *narrative material with powerful encoded themes*. The latter reveal the compelling, personally selected, unconscious perceptions of the meanings of, and conflicts caused by, the prevailing frame-related trigger. In the absence of these two elements, the therapist must remain silent and respect the patient's *communicative defences*.

There are, however, two exceptions to this rule. The first applies to frame impingements that have occurred since the previous session. Because patients almost never mention such incidents— for example, a coincidental meeting between a patient and therapist outside the office, a telephone call from the patient to the therapist or vice versa—clinical observation supports the precept that under these conditions, the therapist can, at a suitable juncture, introduce the missing trigger. This is best done *by using the narrative themes that bridge to the unmentioned trigger* as a lead into a direct reference to the frame-related issue, and then interpreting the patient's encoded perceptions of the therapist in light of the previously omitted triggering event. To complete the intervention, the patient's unconscious processing of the trigger is then articulated, including available models of rectification and evoked conscious and unconscious fantasies and memories.

Ms Bart was in psychotherapy with Ms Terry. On the day after a session, the two women passed each other on the street and said hello to each other. In the next session, Ms Bart said nothing of this brief encounter. She did, however, report a dream in which she is being followed by a female detective, but has no idea why. In associating, she recalled an incident in which her mother had been mugged on the street by a woman who stole her purse.

The patient told other stories, engaged unsuccessfully in various speculations about the trigger that she was trying to work over, and commented that getting things clear in therapy is difficult; she made no allusion to seeing the therapist outside her office. About two-thirds into the session, Ms Bart told a fresh story about a girlfriend who had run into a former homosexual lover on the street and was terrified that the woman would assault her because their break-up had been extremely nasty.

Ms Terry intervened and said that Ms Bart was referring again to an unpleasant meeting with a woman on the street, much as she had done earlier in describing her dream of being followed by a woman detective and in recounting the story of her mother being mugged by a woman. These allusions to incidents and meetings between women on the street must refer to the fact that she and Ms Terry had seen each other on the street last week. In this light, the themes in her dream and stories indicate that Ms Bart had experienced herself as being followed by Ms Terry for no apparent reason and had seen the meeting as sexually seductive and assaultive.

Ms Bart acknowledged the incident and wondered how she could have forgotten it. She then had another association to her dream. The detective looked like a friend of hers who is a brilliant scientist; she does research on the brain and knows a lot about the human mind.

Ms Bart's failure during this session to allude to or remember seeing her therapist on the street is the result of the excessive strength of *conscious system repression* mobilized in response to her therapist's frame deviation—even though the frame break was inadvertent. Evidently fearful of the unconscious experiences that these deviant events arouse, patients are inclined to spare themselves and their therapists direct reports of the disturbing qualities of these shared moments of frame modification. They also are reluctant to provide a direct reference to the frame-deviant trigger and to generate the encoded themes that would enable the therapist to interpret their deep unconscious perceptions of this type of deviation. The absence of a direct allusion to the triggering event is a critical *communicative defence* (Langs, 1997), and it enables the patient to exclude both conscious and deep unconscious reactions to the frame-modifying trigger from the therapeutic dialogue.

In this instance, the therapist used the patient's *bridging theme* of an encounter between two women on the street to initiate her interpretation. She did so at a point in the session where it seemed clear that, despite abundant encoded allusions to the women interacting and meeting on the street, the patient was not manifestly going to mention seeing the therapist on the street. The response to this defence-overriding interpretation included both conscious recall of the incident and subsequent encoded validation of the intervention.

Note, too, that because the meeting was accidental, there was no model of rectification in Ms Bart's material in that there was no way that Ms Terry could secure the frame in this regard (the incident had occurred in a part of the city where neither of them worked or lived). Had the two women met at a health club at which they both were members, the therapist would have been obligated to give up her membership in the club in order to rectify what might otherwise create repetitive frame-breaking contacts between patient and therapist. We can be certain that the patient's encoded imagery would convey this recommendation to the therapist.

The second exception to the rule that the therapist should have both a manifestly represented trigger and powerful encoded themes before interpreting also arises when a direct allusion to the active frame-related triggering event is missing. In this type of incident, the triggering event has transpired in the prior or an earlier session and the patient's failure to mention it directly in the current session is a reflection of very strong obliterating defences. Under these circumstances, were the therapist to intervene and allude to the trigger, the patient's likely response would be one of denial, intellectualizing, and non-validation.

In the presence of a major frame-deviating or frame-securing intervention, a technique has been discovered that often facilitates the patient's recall of this type of missing trigger so that a complete interpretation can eventually be made. Called *a playback of encoded derivatives organized around an unmentioned trigger* (Langs, 1992), the therapist begins this type of intervention with a *bridge to therapy*, a coincidental or general reference by the patient to the treatment situation or therapist. Stating that the patient has mentioned the therapy, the therapist then goes on to play back to the patient the encoded themes relevant to the unmentioned trigger, organizing them around the most thinly disguised representation (descriptive encoded image) of the unmentioned trigger available in the material.

This type of intervention is especially useful when the encoded themes have *power* (i.e. themes of illness, harm, death—the damage package—and, secondarily, those of overt sexuality). *Power themes* are indicators of deep unconscious activity (the system deals only with extremely disturbing, repressed, and denied events and issues) and of conscious system defensiveness.

Playbacks of derivatives find validation either through the patient's subsequent manifest allusion to the trigger or through encoded themes that extend the therapist's and patient's understanding of the repressed frame issue.

To illustrate, had Ms Terry chosen not to mention the missing triggering event, her intervention would have gone something like this:

"You just commented that getting things clear in therapy is difficult, so therapy is on your mind [the general allusion to therapy]. You've brought up several stories about unexpected incidents between women that happened on the street [the theme that best bridges from the narratives to the omitted trigger], and your images touch on being followed, being mugged by a woman, and meeting a former homosexual lover [it is essential to allude to all of the power themes]. These themes must in some way have something to do with something that has happened in connection with you and me and your therapy."

The initial validating response to this kind of intervention is, as noted, the patient's sudden recall of the triggering event. This results from a modification of conscious system repression and facilitates a complete interpretation of the patient's deep unconscious experience of the deviant-frame interlude and increases the possibility of subsequent deep unconscious, encoded validation.

The importance of narratives

Encoded themes—disguised, derivative images—related to the status of frames and framing activities almost always emerge through patients' narratives. These stories have two sets of meanings—one that is consciously intended, and the other that is encoded to reflect unconscious perceptions of the therapist's interventions, with a concentration on frame-related triggers. In contrast, general descriptions, intellectualizations, and ruminations tend to be single-meaning communications without a notable deep unconscious dimension. Furthermore, while direct comments about frame-related issues tend to be sparse, shallow, and unreliable, indirect, encoded comments tend to be multidimensional (they deal with a variety of meanings and perspectives), incisive, and directed towards secured-frame-management efforts.

Stories of all kinds—usually, although not always, about events outside therapy—encode patients' unconscious perceptions and deep unconscious processing of frame-related events. These stories embody both the selectively experienced meanings of frame impingements and, when the frame has been modified, encoded advice as to how the situation can best be rectified.

Sensitivity to *frame-related themes* is a vital asset of a psychotherapist. Because the essential ground rules are limited in number and touch on selected aspects of human needs, *there are a finite number of identifiable frame-relevant themes* that can appear in the narrative-imagery from patients. On the secured-frame side, themes of enclosures, entrapment, the inevitability of death, and sound holding are most common, and their appearance in patients' material should alert the therapist to an active frame-securing intervention (they are easily missed by both patient and therapist). In the presence of such themes, the goal is to discover exactly how the frame has been held secure in face of pressures to modify it, or the means by which an active frame-securing intervention has been made by the patient or therapist.

With regard to frame modifications, the potential themes are constrained by the possible areas of frame impingement. Issues related to frame-deviant settings are reflected in themes of inappropriate or compromised locales, spaces, rooms, and the like; modifications in the time, length, and frequency of sessions are encoded through dysfunctional temporal allusions, references to broken schedules, changed appointments, and the like; fee changes are reflected in stories about manipulating money, greed, stealing, financial exploitation, and the like; modifications in the therapist's relative anonymity evokes themes of exposure, nudity, and such; non-neutral interventions such as directives call forth images of over-controlling and domineering people; and violations of privacy and confidentiality evoke themes of betrayal, exposure, intruders, inappropriate third parties to situations and dyadic relationships, and the inappropriate revelation of personal secrets by an outsider to a relationship.

With time, the therapist who understands the importance of frame-related transactions will develop an inner catalogue of frame-related themes that automatically alerts him or her to the existence of an active framing issue.

The role of power

The human mind denies and represses entire anxiety-provoking and depressing events, as well as many of the most disturbing meanings of remembered traumatic events. This process of obliteration begins at the perceptual level, where many aspects of incidents and evident meanings fail to impact or register consciously. These troublesome impingements are nevertheless received by the human mind through *subliminal or unconscious perception* and then processed outside awareness by the deep unconscious system of the emotion-processing mind.

Unconscious perception is, then, a primary mode of experience when environmental inputs are traumatic and therefore powerful emotionally. This means that the encoded reflections of the perception and processing of these inputs should themselves have considerable power. *Meaningful material contains power themes,* without which an effective intervention on the deep unconscious level is impossible.

The key set of power themes is, as noted, known as *the damage package* because it embodies themes related to death, illness, injury, harm, and the like. Frame-wise, these themes reflect the damaging and persecutory aspects of deviant ground rules on the one hand, and on the other, the universal existential death anxieties aroused by secured frames. In the deviant situation, the damage themes reflect the actual harm to the patient being caused by the therapist, while in the context of a secured frame, damage themes communicate the existential death anxieties that are inevitably evoked by secured and therefore entrapping situations. Clinically, deviant-frame damage themes emerge unqualified, while secured-frame themes of threat are always accompanied by positive themes that reflect the healing aspects of the stable frame.

Overtly sexual themes are the second type of power theme. They have several different underlying structures. As responses to *frame-securing interventions,* they arise firstly, in patients who have suffered incestuous types of seductions, and the themes express a mistrust and dread of people who seem to be trustworthy. They also appear as a manic-denial type of defence against the existential death anxieties aroused by stabilized frames. Nevertheless, on the whole, overt sexual themes are relatively rare under secured-frame conditions, mainly because the stable frame offers clear interpersonal boundaries and functions to de-instinctualize patients' experiences of their therapists and their interventions.

As for *frame modifications*, sexual themes reflect the inappropriately seductive aspects of all frame alterations. They are also activated as manic-denial defences against the predatory, harm-related death anxieties caused by frame modifications. This function of sexual imagery—and of sexual acting out in the everyday life of the patient—can best be understood by realizing that *the emotion-processing mind has evolved primarily to adapt to trauma and death, and the anxieties that they arouse.* The invocation of sexual actions and themes mainly serves psychological defence in that the celebration of sexuality functions adaptively to deny death and death anxieties. In general, the emergence of blatant sexual themes and open sexual feelings towards a therapist should prompt the therapist to search for a recent frame-modifying intervention—deviant frames are the most common contexts for such happenings.

Finally, themes that pertain to events and activities that are impossible or improbable in reality—so-called *mini-psychotic themes*—are indicators that a powerful frame impingement has occurred. The necessity here is for the therapist to search for the triggering event that has activated these themes by engaging in a conscious review of known frame-related triggers, and, if this fails, by processing the themes in the patient's stories for encoded clues to the missing triggering event. Allusions to unrealistic events suggest the presence of a trigger that has deeply disturbed the patient, driven him or her crazy in some way, and elicited deep unconscious perceptions of the therapist as crazy as well. Given the psychotic qualities of this deep unconscious experience, indications are that the evocative triggering event has prompted severe, psychotic-like anxieties in the patient. As a result, the underlying, disruptive, frame-related triggering event is difficult to discover, interpret, and rectify if needed.

Clinical variations

As I have been emphasizing, attention to encoded frame themes is a critical aspect of a therapist's listening and formulating. When a ground rule has been held fast in the face of efforts to modify it or

when it has, instead, been modified, several possible circumstances may exist that will affect how the therapist intervenes.
They involve who is aware of the frame-related trigger and the
possibilities are as follows.

1. *The trigger is known to both parties*

In this first type of situation, both patient and therapist are
consciously aware of the active framing intervention that is at
issue. With the trigger mentioned by the patient and known by
both parties, the therapeutic work is concentrated on the encoded
derivatives conveyed in the patient's narrative material. The
trigger is used to organize the themes—which must have power—
into a cogent understanding of the personally selected, deeply
unconscious meanings that the framing event has had for the
patient.

When the material permits, the themes are interpreted as the
patient's unconscious experience of the triggering event, and,
where needed, rectification follows based on the patient's encoded
derivatives. Often, a frame modification will have unconsciously
evoked a symptom, inappropriate action, or interpersonal distur-
bance in the patient—so-called *symptomatic-patient-indicators* (indications of a patient's need for the therapist to intervene). When
this is the case, the frame-related interpretation is used to explain
the deep unconscious basis of the patient's emotional dysfunction.
From there, depending on the patient's further material, the intervention will extend into other areas such as genetic connections—
early life incidents and such—that have been recalled because they
are connected with the present frame issue. Encoded validation of
these interventions must materialize for a therapist to be satisfied
that he or she has carried out a sound piece of therapeutic work. In
its absence, reformulation is called for. Most often, the problem
lies with the therapist's having selected the wrong trigger for intervening—that is, a more powerful triggering event has been
overlooked by the therapist.

Dr Green, a recently married male therapist, wore his new
wedding ring to a session with Mrs Thomas, who noticed it as
soon as she sat down in her chair. She congratulated her thera-

pist on his marriage and wished him good luck. Soon after, she told a story about John, one of the men where she works, who was sent by the company for counselling because he'd been exposing his genitals to the women employees. If he didn't get his exhibitionism under control, he was going to be fired.

The trigger here was known to both the patient and the therapist: the wearing of the wedding ring. This action is a modification of the ground rule that calls for a therapist's relative anonymity—it is a rule-forbidden self-revelation. This frame impingement registered consciously in the patient's mind, and the *conscious* meanings attached to it were positive—it was seen as a reflection of a happy event. The patient's conscious mind had no appreciation for the frame-modifying qualities and meanings of her therapist's wearing the ring.

Manifest-content therapists would restrict themselves to these surface meanings and would fail to appreciate the frame-deviant aspects of this trigger; they would not interpret its deeply unconscious meanings for the patient. Instead, they would believe, for example, that the patient had, in the session described above, shifted her focus away from the ring and had begun to express exhibitionistic transference fantasies and related sexual conflicts.

This formulation—and any variant that would see this material as involving the fantasies or projections of the patient—turns reality on its head. The therapist's exhibitionistic issues are attributed to the patient. The therapist's offer of such an interpretation might well be accepted *consciously* by the patient, but her *deep unconscious system* would object strongly to the intervention, and these objections would be reflected in encoded themes of people who do not know themselves and who accuse others of their own faults.

Ms Thomas' personally selected, valid deep unconscious experience of this frame-deviant trigger was that the therapist had exposed himself to her sexually. The sexualization (and aggressivization) of patients' deep unconscious experience of therapists' frame modifications is a universal phenomenon. Later material linked this exposure to the exhibitionistic behaviours of her brother—which her therapist was now repeating in an overtly non-sexual manner that was experienced as sexual on the deep unconscious level. The model of rectification in this case is conveyed in the patient's warning about the exhibitionistic employee, which decodes as: "Take the ring off or I will [want to] quit treatment."

The manifest reference by the patient to the trigger and the emergence of the sexual power theme enables the following interpretation:

"You [the patient] mentioned that I [the therapist] am wearing a wedding ring. Your story about John indicates that you experienced my doing so as an inappropriate, rule-violating, sexual exposure. You're telling me that I should get some counselling so I can appreciate and understand what I've done and will stop doing it—that is, take off the ring. Unless I do it, you will want to fire me—leave therapy. In fact, your story makes it clear that I have indeed exposed myself inappropriately to you, so I will take the ring off immediately and not wear it again."

Both meaning and rectification are defined in the patients' derivatives and are used in the proposed interpretive and frame-securing responses. As noted, every frame modification is experienced as instinctualized in both sexual and aggressive ways; there is no distortion in this unconscious response. The patient has selected the sexually exposing unconscious meaning of the trigger because of childhood traumas related to her brother's exhibitionism with her. The therapist unwittingly has symbolically repeated this earlier trauma in his wearing of the ring. These are all valid deep unconscious perceptions and experiences.

Technically, it is essential that the therapist not restrict himself or herself to interpreting the patient's deep unconscious perceptions of the therapist's frame break. When rectification is encoded in the patient's material, it must, whenever feasible, be carried out by the therapist. The ground rules of therapy always pertain to both understanding and appropriate (frame-securing) actions.

Another patient might tell an encoded story of her father's need to tell the world of his affairs with other women, while still another woman patient might speak of a boyfriend who is afraid to be alone with her and frequently brings another woman along on their dates—the ring unconsciously introduces the therapist's wife into the therapeutic dyad. Each of these encoded meanings involves selected, but reasonable, assessments of the deep unconscious implications of this trigger.

2. *The therapist, but not the patient, is aware of the trigger*

The second kind of therapy situation is one in which the therapist, but not the patient, is aware of an active frame-related triggering event/intervention. Thus, the patient fails to allude to the therapist's framing effort and shows no indication of being aware of it. The encoded themes in the patient's material do, however, reflect and organize around the frame issue in question, be it frame-modifying or frame-securing—attention to the encoded themes is vital here. At an appropriate point in this type of session, when the themes accrue power and represent the trigger with relatively little disguise, the therapist should play back the relevant encoded themes, organizing them around the unmentioned trigger. The goal is to enable the patient, who unconsciously but not consciously knows exactly what the trigger is, to become directly aware of the trigger—and of his or her deep unconscious responses to it.

The results of this kind of intervention depend on the nature of the repressed frame-break or frame-securing activity at issue, the prior and existing conditions of the therapy frame, and the inner state of the patient. When the frame is otherwise secured, there is a strong likelihood that a patient will eventually consciously recover a repressed, deviant triggering event. Patients with a history of few death-related traumas are also more likely to recover a repressed trigger than highly traumatized patients. This aspect of a patient's personal history plays a notable role in this type of situation because the experience of death-related traumas is a key factor in psychic functioning and a major cause of overly defensive reactions to the frame of therapy and framing interventions of the therapist—both frame-securing and frame-modifying.

When the frame has been modified, the particular ground rule that has been violated is also a factor in recovering a repressed intervention. Each compromise of a ground rule has both universal and personal meanings and has an impact on the patient in a manner that combines these two elements. Some meanings of a frame break are relatively easily processed by a given patient, and the trigger is readily rescued from repression when the therapist offers a sound playback of available encoded derivatives. Other meanings are so assaultive and disturbing that the patient maintains his or her communicative, repressive, and denial defences despite all efforts by the therapist.

Triggers with strong death-related ramifications may remain repressed despite the presence of minimally disguised derivatives and the most astute efforts at playback by the therapist. This is common, for example, when a therapist or a third party informs a patient of a serious traumatic incident in the therapist's life—for example, the death or serious illness of a family member. In these situations, the therapist should *not* introduce the repressed trigger, because doing so will be experienced by the patient as assaultive and confessional—and as asking the patient to function as a therapist to the therapist. The result will be conscious rumination and displaced anger, but little working through of the deep unconscious meanings of the patient's experience of the trigger (Langs, 1997). An underlying anxiety-provoking, deep unconscious image of the therapist as a murderer is typical when a member of the therapist's family falls ill or suffers a major accidental death. In addition, the patient's own dread of his or her unresolved death-related issues motivates a need to sustain a strong measure of psychological and communicative defence under these circumstances.

In general, patients' repressions of frame modifications related to the relatively fixed aspects of the frame tend to resolve relatively easily, while violations of privacy and confidentiality evoke greater resistances against the patient's consciously retrieving a trigger that has been subjected to repression. Modifications of the relative anonymity of the therapist, especially when the information is disturbing, can create such extremes of denial and repression that, despite abundant derivative representations and power themes, the patient is unable to become aware of the obliterated triggering event. In some cases, this non-recall is sustained for months or years, even though the encoded imagery persists with great intensity in session after session. The conscious mind is designed to operate with a great deal of perceptual denial and to repress a remarkable number of once consciously registered frame-deviant events.

3. *The patient, but not the therapist, is aware of the trigger*

As a rule, if a patient is aware of a triggering event that the therapist has missed, the patient will, in time, communicate it directly to the therapist, who is thereby alerted to the frame issue at hand. Very rarely, a patient will inadvertently or deliberately conceal a frame issue from the therapist. When this is done consciously, it is a violation of the ground rule that requires the patient to report whatever comes to mind. The most common situation in which this occurs involves a patient who is unconsciously terrified of a secured frame because of severe, early death-related traumas. These patients may keep secret a frame deviation that they have engaged in unilaterally because they are fearful of experiencing the securing of the modified rule. Examples of this kind of problem include unreported third-party contributors to the payment of the fee (paying the fee is entirely the responsibility of the patient), a patient's seeing other emotionally relevant healers in addition to the therapist (the rule is one healer per patient), or a patient's talking to a third party about the therapy (a violation of the privacy and confidentiality of the therapy).

4. *Both patient and therapist are unaware of the trigger*

In the last type of situation, both the patient and the therapist are unaware of an active frame-related triggering event. This circumstance poses an enormous challenge to the therapist who needs to recover from and modify his or her own use of denial and repression—that is, to recover a notable frame-related intervention that he or she has made and then lost to awareness. In most of these instances, the trigger is frame-modifying and the unconscious need in both parties is to sustain the deviant conditions of treatment—underlying secured-frame anxieties are usually a major factor.

Because triggers evoke encoded themes, *the themes in the patient's narratives are clues to the identity of a missing trigger and its meanings*. Thus, the appearance of stories with themes related to one of the ground rules of therapy (e.g. money, exposure, entrapment, incestuous seduction, etc.—see above) should alert the therapist to a missing frame-related triggering event.

Encoded themes indicate, first, whether the trigger is frame-securing or frame-modifying, and, second, the specific type of frame-related intervention involved. Themes that speak for *frame-securing interventions* involve two classes of narratives: those with positive, holding, rule-abiding imagery and those with entrapping imagery, often with annihilatory features. This is in keeping with the dual attributes of frame-securing interventions—they offer inherent support and safety and also arouse existential death anxieties.

Frame modifications are identified through such themes as criminality and breaches of the law, rule-breaking, violations of boundaries, inappropriate intrusions into spaces and lives, unethical behaviours, violations of social mores and contracts, and the like.

As for clues to the particular way in which the frame has been secured or modified, the narrative themes will be in keeping with the ground rule involved. If the fee is at issue, for example, there will be themes related to money. Thus, if the fee was sustained in the face of pressures from the patient to reduce it and the incident then forgotten by both parties, the images will touch on people who know how to handle money and who are able to resist financial corruption. Along different lines, if a third party has been introduced into the therapy by either or both parties, themes of intruders, exposure, spies, and the like will emerge.

These encoded clues to a missing frame-related triggering event are one type of *bridging theme*, a connector that runs from the encoded story to a meaning of the framing intervention—from the manifest image to its encoded, latent meaning. The appearance of repetitive, frame-related bridging themes almost always means that there is an active, unrecognized framing trigger that the patient is unconsciously working over at the moment. These images should prompt the therapist to search the recent past for an overlooked frame impingement that can account for the themes. If direct recall fails to bring forth the missing trigger, the therapist can then, at an appropriate point in a session, offer a playback of the relevant themes, using a general allusion to therapy to connect the themes to the treatment situation. This intervention engages the patient in the pursuit of the missing trigger—both consciously through an effort to recall what has been missed and unconsciously through the production of fresh derivative imagery. The result may be conscious recall of the missing trigger or new and less disguised clues to its identity. In turn, this can help the therapist to modify his or her own defences so that the overlooked trigger can be recovered.

Another type of clue to the existence of a bilaterally repressed frame-related trigger is the expression of *unexplained powerful narrative themes*—for example, the damage package—in a patient's material. Power themes are always evoked by framing triggers, and all such themes should be accounted for by linking them to a known, active trigger. The inability to find such a trigger means that a frame-related intervention has been repressed, and the therapist must then engage in the work described above in an effort to recover the missing trigger. Monitoring the patient's material for frame-related themes is an ever-present task for every psychotherapist and counsellor.

CHAPTER FIVE

Secured and modified frames

I n approaching the definition of secured and modified frames, we may recall some of the differences between the conscious and deep unconscious systems of the emotion-processing mind. The world experienced by the conscious mind is received through conscious perception, and its purview is wide and varied. Concerned with past, present, and future, the system explores and organizes the world along many different dimensions—danger, care, food, shelter, relatedness, sexuality, finances, illness and health, creativity, travel, and so on. Its adaptive resources are applied in enormously diverse ways.

Relying on subliminal perception, the deep unconscious system has its own view and experience of the world. Deep unconscious perception is concentrated intensely on a single dimension of human experience: that related to frames and framing activities—the realm of rules, laws, and boundaries. While the system also monitors the kind of listening and formulating that a therapist engages in (it distinguishes trigger decoders from those working with manifest contents and their implications) and the accuracy of a therapist's interventional efforts, the deep unconscious system is primarily frame-centered.

In the conscious world, there are many ways of dividing up the realm of experience. But in the world experienced by the deep unconscious system, a simple bipartite classification prevails: *frames are either secured or modified*. Deep unconscious experience is, then, divided into a *secured-frame domain* and a *deviant-frame domain*, each with its own distinctive properties, functions, and effects.

In most psychotherapy situations, the conscious mind can make a fair assessment of the status of the frame and decide whether it is secured or deviant. The basic definitions are clear: a secured frame entails adherence to all of the unconsciously validated ground rules described in chapter three, while a deviant frame entails any departure from these ideals.

Only rarely is there some uncertainty consciously regarding this issue. For example, if a patient is late for a session, does the therapist's beginning the session late entail a frame-securing or frame-modifying intervention—or both? The same may be asked of a therapist who resumes a session after the patient has interrupted it to go to the lavatory. The conscious mind may be uncertain as to the answer to these frame-status questions, but the deep unconscious mind is not—in both cases, the therapist's intervention is both frame modifying and frame securing. In any case, it is to be stressed again that *all frame-status evaluations must ultimately rely on and be confirmed by the deeply unconsciously validated trigger decoding of the patient's responsive encoded material as he or she adapts to a frame-related trigger.*

Among the many types of interventions, those that involve framing are most easily assessed. Non-framing verbal interventions are called *impression triggers* because patients' conscious impressions lack precise guidelines and are highly subjective. Beliefs that a given comment was hostile, seductive, controlling, unnecessary, correct, or mistaken are difficult to evidence unambiguously, and the relevant narrative material from patients is especially difficult to assess for unconscious evaluations. In contrast, in most cases a ground rule is established or not, enforced or modified, respected or violated, presently active or absent.

On rare occasions, *the frame may be modified in order to secure or re-secure it*—that is, a frame-related intervention is of a mixed nature. For example, a low fee may be increased—which is an intervention that modifies the ground rule that calls for a fixed fee throughout the course of a therapy, yet it secures the frame by establishing the therapist's regular fee in place of a self-sacrificing, frame-deviant low fee. Still, while a given intervention may have mixed qualities, the overall status of the framework of a therapy is almost always definable as entirely secured or compromised in small or large ways.

As noted, the secured- and deviant-frame domains each have a set of distinctive, universal properties that set them apart. In psychotherapy, the type of basic frame affects the patient's picture of the therapist, the ways in which interventions are experienced, the available mode of cure, the preferred means of coping, the nature of active defences and resistances, the quality of the therapeutic hold and containment, and much more. Most tellingly, *both frame securing and frame modifying are basic approaches to emotional adaptation—humans habitually cope by either adhering to rules and boundaries or violating them*. Frame-related preferences and behaviours are at the core of an individual's adaptive strategies. These coping efforts are, in turn, tellingly connected to a patient's emotional dysfunctions or health; they are regularly utilized in both the therapy itself and in the patient's everyday life.

The two modes of therapy

The distinction between secured and deviant frames leads to the demarcation of two fundamental forms of psychotherapy—*secured-frame therapy* and *deviant-frame therapy*. Based on deep unconscious experience, this classification cuts across all of the other ways of categorizing psychotherapies. On this level, then, psychoanalysis and other dynamic forms of psychotherapy that are structured with modified frames share a great deal with cognitive and supportive therapies whose frames are consistently deviant by deep unconscious standards. Deep unconscious experience is compelling and affecting regardless of the consciously accepted, usual framework of a particular treatment modality.

The type of psychotherapy that a patient will receive, whether frame secured or frame modified, is usually established in the consultation session. Secured-frame therapy arises when the referral and first telephone call are without contaminating factors such as prior personal contact between the patient and therapist or the patient having received personal information about the therapist. Then, in the first session, the therapist defines the ideal ground rules and the patient accepts them, and the treatment unfolds accordingly. Any departure from this ideal creates a deviant-frame mode of therapy.

In the course of treatment, deliberately or inadvertently, consciously and unconsciously, patients repeatedly test the prevailing qualities of the frame and the therapist's ability to sustain as much of the ideal, secured frame as possible. Patients may, for example, either modify a ground rule on their own and await the therapist's reaction, or request a frame modification from the therapist—for example, a change in the time of a particular session or a reduction in the fee. The therapist's response will determine the type of therapy that the patient will then receive. Similarly, if the therapist discovers an overlooked frame modification, the choice must be made to either secure the ground rule or allow it to remain altered. If a ground rule should accidentally be modified by the therapist—for example, an inadvertent extension of a session—the frame can be either re-secured or allowed to continue in a modified form.

In all of these instances, the therapist's response should be based on the patient's encoded directives. Without exception, they will speak for securing the ground rule at issue and for secured-frame therapy. Failure to follow these directives may lead the therapist erroneously to modify the frame or sustain an existing frame deviation. The result is, of course, a frame-modified treatment situation, yet one that may be open to rectification. At times, however, there are frame modifications that cannot be undone or rectified—for example, a patient obtaining personal information about the personal life of the therapist—and these situations pose special problems that will be discussed below.

By design and for purposes of defence, the conscious mind strongly favours deviant rather than secured frames and modes of adaptation. Inadvertent frame breaks and the tendency to overlook existing frame modifications are not infrequent occurrences in the work of the most determined frame-securing therapists. Thus, therapists need to be continuously on the alert for their frame-altering inclinations, interventions, and behaviours and for the repression, avoidance, and denial that typically accompany them.

The secured frame

Secured frames have a group of *universal properties* that affect both patients and therapists, as does every frame-securing moment in an otherwise compromised treatment situation. I turn now to presenting these attributes.

Beneficial aspects

The secured frame inherently supports and protects from harm both patient and therapist, creates an ambience of mutual trust, promotes exploration rather than uncalled-for action, creates and reinforces constructive modes of adaptation, implicitly supports the fulfilment of the valid and constructive role requirements of both parties to therapy, and speaks for a deeply insightful means of resolving a patient's emotional dysfunctions.

The constructive facets of secured frames are the following.

1. *A sense of safety.* For the patient, a secured frame inherently expresses the reliability and trustworthiness of the therapist. It is safe for the patient to communicate both conscious and deep unconscious secrets, including disturbing conscious and unconscious perceptions of the therapist, without fear of criticism or retribution. The patient is assured that the therapist will try to understand these images and not be inclined to retaliate when wounded psychologically by them.

For the therapist, the secured frame provides a backdrop for his or her therapeutic work that speaks for its sincerity and constructive qualities. The ideal frame also makes it safe to interpret and maintain the ground rules as needed, with the expectation that the patient will consistently try to understand the therapist's interpretive and frame-managing efforts, including his or her deviant-frame lapses. In addition, the secured frame curtails patients' impulses to retaliate against their therapists when they offer valid—and even invalid—somewhat hurtful interpretations and frustrating but necessary frame-management interventions.

2. *The provision of clear and appropriate physical and interpersonal boundaries.* The secured frame establishes a strong and appropriate set of interpersonal boundaries between patients and therapists, both physical and mental, thereby protecting both parties from uncalled-for physical and psychological intrusions, assaults, or seductions. The patient's sense of personal integrity and self-esteem are thereby supported.

For the therapist, the secured frame creates the conditions for deeply empathic identifications with the patient, with the assurance that this will occur in a limited manner and without danger of a shift to an action mode. In all, the clear boundaries of secured-frame therapy facilitate interactions in which interpersonal and psychological boundaries may be momentarily lost for therapeutic purposes and then quickly restored.

3. *A devotion to the therapeutic needs of the patient and a renunciation of inappropriate emotional needs by both patient and therapist.* The secured frame ensures a focus in psychotherapy, consciously and deeply unconsciously, on the patient's psychopathology, interpersonal dysfunctions, and other maladaptations. At the same time, it protects both the patient from seeking inappropriate satisfactions from the therapist, and the therapist from imposing or gratifying his or her countertransference-based needs at the expense of the patient.

4. *A mode of cure that avoids maladaptive forms of action-discharge and is essentially based on trigger-decoded insights and positive frame-management efforts.* Adherence to the ideal ground rules is the best possible means of minimizing patients' and therapists' inclinations to seek cure through maladaptive forms of action-discharge, a mode that always involves modifying frames within and/or outside therapy. Secured frames create conditions for a "talking cure" that is supported by the benefits of sound holding for both parties to therapy. Furthermore, *secured frames speak for a basic mode of adaptation* that involves thought, planning, appropriate action, a

minimization of unnecessary harm to self and others, and tolerance of inevitable anxieties such as existential death anxiety.

5. *A sound relationship with the therapist in the form of a healthy symbiosis.* The secured frame ensures that the therapeutic relationship is appropriately tilted so that the patient obtains the greater share of gratification and cure. He or she does so by accepting and working over the therapist's sound frame-management efforts and unconsciously validated trigger-decoded interpretations. The therapist's satisfactions are limited to those that come from contributing to the cure of the patient and thereby respectably earning a living.

Departures from the ideal frame always introduce the therapist's countertransferences into the treatment situation. Unconsciously, at such interludes the therapist functions as a patient asking for help and the patient is forced into the role, however unknowingly, of the therapist. The relationship then becomes a pathological symbiosis or a parasitism of the patient.

6. *Inherent support for the patient's and the therapist's sense of self and identity, and their ego, id, and superego functioning.* The secured frame enhances all aspects of a patient's self-image, functioning, mental health, and adapting. This frame bolsters reality testing because the therapist, as promised, functions as a therapist. Also enhanced are the patient's capacity to relate, make use of sound psychological, communicative, and physical defences, seek appropriate satisfactions, and enhance the operation of other ego functions. This frame also supports reasonable superego standards, effective self-regulation, as well as healthy ways of satisfying and sublimating raw sexual and aggressive impulses and needs. These enhancements are transmitted through the inherent properties of the secured frame and the patient's introjective identifications with a therapist capable of establishing and maintaining this difficult-to-sustain framework throughout a psychotherapy.

7. *The positive reinforcement of the beneficial effects of the therapist's unconsciously validated interpretations.* A therapist's offer of a secured frame supports and does not contradict interpretive healing efforts. The two basic interventions available to a therapist—valid interpretations and securing the frame—go hand in hand as the optimal means of helping patients to resolve adaptively their emotional difficulties. Properly executed, this con-

cordance spares the therapist highly disruptive forms of *unconscious guilt* caused by his or her own deep unconscious perceptions of the hurtful qualities of modifying the frame or intervening erroneously.

Overall, a secured frame is inherently healing for both parties to therapy, and in many cases accounts for much of a patient's cure. Securing frames is a fundamental mode of adaptation with remarkably positive effects. The secured frame and secured-frame moments in the course of a deviant-frame therapy are the hallmarks of truly effective psychotherapy.

Sources of anxiety

The healing powers of secured frames and frame-securing moments are immense and well established. We therefore must ask why, despite strong evidence and ample deep unconscious protests, are most patients inclined consciously to seek or accept a psychotherapy that departs from these health-giving ideals? Why, too, are so few therapists prepared to do everything they can to offer such frames to their patients? Why does the conscious system—the manager of our choices and the seat of conscious perceptions—generally prefer modifying to securing frames, and why does it fail to see the harm that both patients and therapists suffer under these conditions?

A large part of the answer to these questions lies with the *death anxieties* that are evoked by secured frames in all humans—patients and therapists alike (Langs, 1997). The essential qualities of the secured frame are not unlike life itself. Life is our greatest gift, yet it ends in our greatest personal disaster—death. Similarly, the secured frame, which is the greatest "gift" that a therapist can give to a patient, evokes the most dreadful form of death anxiety that humans experience—*existential death anxiety*.

The disturbing features of the secured frame evidently outweigh their potential healing attributes for the conscious minds of most patients and therapists. Let us examine why.

1. *The optimal set of ground rules is restrictive and limiting.* The secured frame calls for a closed and private setting that isolates the patient and therapist from the rest of the world, thereby arousing

the basic interpersonal mistrust and paranoid anxieties of both parties to therapy. This frame, for example, insists on a firm commitment from both members of the therapeutic dyad with respect to being at the same place at the same time, for the same length of time, week after week. This claustrum-like experience activates claustrophobic anxieties and fears of commitment, entrapment, and isolation.

2. *Humans tend to prefer active adaptations and defences; thus the relative immobility of the patient and therapist within secured frames arouses feelings and fears of passivity and of being overwhelmed emotionally by the other party to the therapy.* Active responsiveness, which offers the illusion of a realistic sense of mastery, tends to be preferred by most individuals to passive contemplation, delay, and planning. Humans experience immobility as rendering them vulnerable to predatory harm and therefore tend to dread a frame that curtails active responsiveness. Deviant-frame therapies always entail activities on the part of one or both parties to a therapy, but they are maladaptive and emotionally detrimental.

3. *The claustrum-like effects of the secured frame evoke intense forms of existential death anxiety that are usually experienced outside of awareness.* Secured-frame death anxieties, strongly linked to the recognition of the inevitability of personal demise, render these frames difficult to endure—despite their very positive effects. Basically, secured frames are linked unconsciously to the realization that we are all trapped in a living space from which we depart or escape only through death.

Patients and therapists are strongly inclined to defend themselves at all costs against these anxieties, which they believe will overwhelm and annihilate them psychologically. They appear to be convinced unconsciously that existential death anxiety cannot be mastered and must therefore be dealt with through denial and avoidance—defences that are inherent properties of modified frames. This lack of faith seen in humans regarding the likelihood of successfully adapting to issues and anxieties related to the inevitability of death is a major cause of the frame-deviant havoc that exists today in both psychotherapy and the world at large.

4. *The secured frame deprives both patients and therapists of their usual modes of pathological gratification and their customary defences against death anxiety and against higher level conflicts related to sexual-*

ity, aggression, and self-image. Both patients and therapists are invested in a variety of maladaptive modes of satisfaction and denial-based defences against death anxiety, including the use of frame-modifying actions; these behaviours are, of course, difficult to sustain within secured frames. Personal growth and insightful conflict resolution can be effectively accomplished only when these maladaptive inclinations are curtailed. Nevertheless, the loss of these modes of protection poses threats that both patients and therapists find difficult to tolerate.

A primary *selection factor* in the evolution of the emotion-processing mind has been the language-based realization that all humans must die. Dealing with existential and some measure of predatory death anxieties is the fundamental or archetypical emotionally charged adaptive task for all humans. Denial-based defences—of which there are many variants, including modifying frames—appear to be the primary evolved means of protection that patients and therapists invoke unconsciously when dealing with death-related issues—and they do so regardless of the cost to themselves and others (Langs, 1996, 1997).

In all, then, this preference for defence through frame modification joins forces with the anxieties evoked by the death-related, entrapping qualities of the secured frame to motivate most patients and therapists to prefer modified to secured frames. One of the greatest challenges facing every therapist and counsellor today lies with overcoming their evolved and personally defensive needs for modified frames so that they can offer and effectively manage the secured frames that both they and their patients so greatly need.

The modified frame

The modified frame is defined as any therapeutic setting or contract in which one or more of the unconsciously validated, basic ground rules is compromised. *Deviant frame therapy* is defined as any therapy in which one or more of the ideal ground rules is absent from the basic framework of the treatment.

Frame-modifying moments, which are inevitable in every psychotherapy, are those interludes in which either the patient or the therapist, or both, alter an ideal ground rule of therapy. These breaks may occur in the context of an essentially secured frame or in one that is fundamentally deviant—the background frame conditions will affect the patient's response to the immediate deviation. Frame modifications in the course of a therapy may be temporary and rectifiable, or extended and unrectifiable except by terminating the therapy. When a frame deviation is uncorrectable, its effects can be lessened by refraining from further frame modifications of any kind.

The costly relief offered by frame modifications

The advantages of deviant frames are realized in emotionally costly maladaptations that have detrimental consequences that tend to be overlooked or denied by patients and therapists alike. Among the *maladaptive gains* derived from a modified frame, the following are notable.

1. *The avoidance of secured-frame death and other anxieties.* Patients obtain this relief at the cost of not dealing with or resolving their existential death anxieties, which are the fundamental anxieties of life and living. No psychotherapy is complete without an exploration of these anxieties and without enabling a patient to find the means of coping better with them. Thus, all modified-frame therapies should have frame-securing moments in which an altered ground rule is rectified or a secured ground rule is maintained in the face of pressures to alter it. These *secured-frame interludes* account for much of the sound healing in deviant-frame therapies.

2. *The reinforcement of pathological defences against death-related and other types of conflict and anxieties.* Modified frames are enactments that are constituted as maladaptive and harmful uses of defensive behaviours that tend to reflect a basic mode of adaptation that precludes the development of more effective ways of coping emotionally. These defences have distinct manic, action-discharge, and denial qualities, and they readily lead to destructive forms of acting out within and outside therapy. They also

obstruct true growth and the achievement of genuine insight and inner peace.

3. *The reduction of communicated narratives that encode the patient's unconscious experiences, especially those that are related to the frame and his or her emotional difficulties.* Derivatives are communicative compromises that express but disguise unconscious perceptions of therapists' interventions and the deep unconscious processing of their meanings. As such, they are a potential source of deep insight and of guidelines to the proper management of the ground rules, but they are also anxiety-provoking. Modifications of the ground rules signal the danger of encoded images and favour the patient's use of denial and communicative resistances and non-expression. As a form of action-discharge, frame modifications motivate patients to *act maladaptively* rather than *adaptively engage in encoding through narratives*—the vehicles for unconscious meaning that facilitates the development of deep insight.

4. *The satisfactions of pathological forms of relatedness.* The parties to a deviant frame are engaged in either a pathological symbiosis or a parasitic interaction in which exploitation, inappropriate seduction and merger, and aggressive discharge are enacted. Nevertheless, patients are attracted to this kind of relatedness not only because of the maladaptive satisfactions involved, but also because of their strong sense of guilt for their misdeeds, real and imagined, and their resultant need for punishment from their therapists. *Unconscious guilt* is a powerful factor in both patients and therapists in motivating them to accept modified frames and the harm that they cause.

5. *A sense of relief for the patient effected through deep unconscious nefarious comparisons with the frame-modifying therapist.* The therapist who compromises the frame is unconsciously perceived by the patient as dysfunctional and unable to manage his or her impulses and needs. As a result, the patient experiences a sense of relief because these perceptions, even though they are unconscious, place the patient in a favourable light compared to the therapist. The therapist's frame alterations are seen as acts of madness, and the patient unconsciously feels reassured that he or she is not as disturbed as the therapist.

The cost of deviating

Frame modifications exact their toll emotionally and often play a role in patients' symptomatic remissions and acting out, in stalemated therapies, and in adverse events in the life of therapists. Their harmful qualities are consistently alluded to in patients' encoded responses to specific frame-deviant interventions. The main drawbacks of frame modifications are, then, as follows:

1. They establish frame-breaking as a patient's *modus operandi* and preferred means of adapting. When conflicts and anxieties are activated, patients in frame-deviant forms of therapy will be inclined to attempt to adapt via further frame modifications— in the therapy and/or in their daily lives.

2. They support pathological defences, modes of relating, and gaining satisfaction and relief, and general inclinations toward maladaptive responsiveness to activated triggers.

3. They preclude the expression of the vital encoded narratives that are needed to interpret a patient's deep unconscious world of experience. The unavailability of deep unconscious resourcefulness entails a loss of important adaptive capabilities.

4. They deprive patients of the inherent safety, support, and ego-enhancement that they are entitled to from a psychotherapist.

5. They are inherently persecutory, exploitative, and inappropriately seductive acts that arouse the patient's paranoid and predatory death anxieties.

6. For deviant-frame therapists, there is a strong likelihood that the quality of their lives will be greatly compromised because of the *deep unconscious guilt* that they experience as a result of unconscious self-perceptions of the harm that they cause their patients.

In light of the damage that they cause—and it includes suicide and homicide—the human preference for deviant frames is grim testimony to the basic flaws in the architecture and operations of the emotion-processing mind, which, as a language-based entity, has had a mere 150,000 years to evolve (Langs, 1996). To a great extent, effective psychotherapy entails overcoming the basic maladaptive configuration and functioning of the human emotion-processing mind. Frame breaking may be thought of as an endemic human disease—a silent, unnoticed, genetically orchestrated plague that is wreaking havoc with patients, therapists, and people the world over.

The unrectifiable frame

A notable problem arises in situations in which a frame modification cannot be undone or rectified. Self-revelations, for example, cannot be erased from a patient's mind; the referral of a patient by another patient of the same therapist is uncorrectable; and a prior relationship between a patient and therapist cannot be undone. These kinds of frame modifications create a permanent deviant cast to, and major problems throughout, a psychotherapy.

In some cases, the unrectifiable frame deviation undermines the therapy. The patient is unable to feel secure or to trust the therapist. Exploitative and seductive unconscious perceptions of the therapist prevail, and self-harmful acting out by these patients is all but unavoidable. In these *unrectifiable deviant-frame therapies*, the therapeutic work should be *geared towards an insightful termination of the therapy*—a course of action that will be orchestrated by the patient's deep unconscious derivatives.

On the other hand, if the unmodifiable frame deviation involves a single event or does not appear to be interfering with the ongoing, validated therapeutic work, and the remainder of the frame is secured and the deviation will not be repeated, it is possible to offer a patient a viable treatment experience. At present, this type of *limited frame-deviant/otherwise frame-secured therapy* is justified in locales and situations where a suitable alternative therapy is not available to the patient.

Much of this applies in principle to clinic and managed-care forms of treatment and with patients for whom an ideally framed psychotherapy is not possible. In the private sector, a patient may be seeing a frame-sensitive therapist under deviant-frame conditions and may find that another therapist with this capability is not available in the area. Under these circumstances, it is usually best for the patient to have the benefit of working with a frame-sensitive therapist in a modified treatment situation rather than with a frame-insensitive, frame-breaking therapist. The harm caused by the unrectifiable frame deviation in the existing therapy will be pitted against the healing powers of the secured aspects of the remainder of the frame. In general, when properly interpreted and managed, healing will win out.

Modified and secured frames: a clinical excerpt

The following vignette illustrates many of the issues discussed in this chapter.

> Ms Jensen, a woman in her early 30s, called Dr Porter, a male therapist, for a consultation. When asked by the therapist how she got his name, Ms Jensen said that her minister had recommended him to her. The therapist offered a time for the consultation that the patient was able to use, gave her his address, and the call was ended.

> In the first part of the consultation session, Ms Jensen described her main complaints as bowel symptoms, which had been labelled psychosomatic, and difficulties in relating to men, from whom she tended to shy away. She told the therapist that she liked being alone and found considerable comfort when she is in her apartment reading and listening to music. She admitted that in her solitude she gets scared at times and has trouble breathing, but most of the time being home alone is fine with her.

> She next spoke of a very tentative relationship with a man she was seeing and then of her job in marketing for a publishing house. In her work, she is under pressure from an endless stream of intruders, including people to whom she gives business. They ply her with gifts that are something like bribes. This makes doing her job almost impossible and causes her to run to the bathroom over and over again.

At this point in the hour, Ms Jensen asked Dr Porter if he accepted insurance coverage. She explained that she couldn't possibly afford his fee on the salary that she was earning and added that she was quite comfortable in using the insurance. Dr Porter responded by suggesting Ms Jensen continue to say whatever came to mind.

The patient paused and then said that she was thinking of an incident at work that had happened earlier that week. She was in the bathroom—it's unisex—and she had inadvertently left the door unlocked. The chief editor of her company, a married man whom she found very attractive, had walked in on her. She was horribly embarrassed and speechless for a moment. He just laughed and kidded her by saying that this was a pretty strange way to seduce a man—was she trying to turn a trick? He just stood there and stared at her, and an image flashed through her mind that he was hiding a knife and was about to murder her. She then screamed and sent him off. She couldn't concentrate for the rest of the day. She was furious with herself for leaving herself open to that kind of exposure.

To formulate the material to this point, the referral here was frame-secured because it was made by a helping professional and did not involve personal revelations about the therapist. Also, the telephone call was handled in a secure manner, and Dr Porter's private office was frame-secured. The patient's experience of these sound-frame qualities is reflected in her first narrative about her feelings of security when she is at home alone with a book and some music. The allusion to having trouble breathing suggests a measure of secured-frame anxiety as well.

The material then shifted towards negative imagery, whose main themes were those of intrusion, gifts, and bribes—all with detrimental consequences. Because the request that the therapist accept a third-party payer followed these images, Ms Jensen appears to have been encoding her unconscious perceptions of Dr Porter were he to accept payment from the insurance company. In light of this *anticipated trigger*, her responsive encoded themes to this point indicate that his doing so would be experienced by her as an intrusion—the introduction of a third party into the therapy—and as allowing her to bribe him.

The patient then announced the anticipated trigger, affording it a manifest representation. This particular trigger would modify the basic structure of the therapy through departures from the ideal ground rules related to the patient's full responsibility for the payment of the fee, total privacy, and total confidentiality.

The narrative that followed centred on themes of exposure, sexual seductiveness, prostitution, and money. We may take the allusion to *money* as the *bridging theme* that connects the *encoded story* with *the anticipated frame-related trigger*. The story decodes around the trigger in this way:

> "If you [the therapist] accept payment from the insurance company it will expose me [the patient] inappropriately, create a seductive atmosphere, and make you into a prostitute. We should keep out the intruder, and if one is allowed in, he or she should be removed from this space as soon as possible or I will leave therapy. The presence of the third party renders me speechless [i.e. it will lead to the relative absence of encoded material]."

Notice that upon announcing the frame-related trigger, the deep unconscious system immediately created a narrative with valid unconscious perceptions of the actual meanings of the anticipated frame break. Consciously, the patient wanted to use her insurance and was comfortable with this frame modification, but deeply unconsciously she did not want it at all. *This conflict reflects the most common split in the emotion-processing mind—a conscious system that favours frame breaking pitted against a deep unconscious system that opposes it.* We also see again that the conscious system is in control of the patient's actual behaviours, even as the deep unconscious system reveals through encoded narratives how destructive it would be. In the emotional domain, humans routinely act against their own best interests—*deep unconscious wisdom has no access or palpable effects on conscious adaptations.*

The potential frame break was experienced as both seductive and murderous: it aroused strong predatory death anxieties in the patient. There were also feelings of embarrassment and humiliation, and a sense of dishonesty (prostitution, bribe) and manipulation. The patient's striking deep unconscious view of the traumatic qualities of the frame modification stands in contrast to her benign conscious view.

The material also indicates that, without consciously being aware of it, Ms Jensen inherently possesses a deep unconscious model of the secured frame and an appreciation for the consequences of departing from the ideal framework of a psychotherapy. Such deep unconscious wisdom is a universal attribute of the human emotion-processing mind, which appears to possess an evolved, inherited frame-sensitive mental module that unfortunately lacks the mental tracts through which we could draw upon that wisdom for direct, conscious adaptation.

If we take at face value the patient's claim that she is unable to afford the therapist's expected fee, we are confronted with a major problem for the field of psychotherapy today. Therapists are loathe to price themselves out of availability for many patients, as well they should be. But, nevertheless, regardless of conscious need and concern, a frame break has a variety of inevitable negative effects, and these detrimental consequences cannot be denied away—they are very real, even when they are necessary and go unnoticed.

The best a therapist can do under these circumstances is to limit the therapy to one session per week and allow the patient to determine whether there is any way that he or she can afford the therapist's customary fee. If not, the fee can be reduced in the hope that the patient can work over the deviant meanings and effects of this frame modification and be in a position to benefit from therapy. To do so, the frame would need to be secure enough in other ways to allow for encoded responses to the reduced fee and for their interpretation. Ideally, the patient will at some point find a way to earn more money, and the frame can then be modified to secure it. If not, the therapy may move towards *an unrectifiable frame modification-termination type of therapy* in which the encoded themes will take the patient through an insightful ending to the treatment experience. In all cases, it is essential that, as much as possible, the therapist avoids any other frame modifications in the therapy.

These are difficult situations for the therapist because, despite all necessity, the patient's unconscious perceptions are often of being harmed in devastating ways. In addition, if the negative consequences of the frame break are recognized consciously, there is *conscious guilt* for the therapist to deal with. More ominous are situations in which the therapist is unaware consciously of the effects of the frame modification that he or she has created and fails to appreciate the patient's deep unconscious experience of it. This causes considerable *deep unconscious guilt,* which may then prompt the therapist to act out in self-defeating ways in his or her professional and social lives. Modifying a frame of therapy even for humanistic reasons can cause havoc and harm despite all good intentions—therapists should proceed cautiously under these circumstances.

CHAPTER SIX

Frames
and the evolution
of the two-system mind

Throughout physical and biological nature, rules, frames, and boundaries have played a critical role in how entities, systems, and organisms function, interact, and survive. For organisms, frames and boundaries provide contexts and limits for behaviour and experienced meaning, while rules and laws guide adaptations and interactions.

In general, animals and other species respect these guidelines. Within the boundaries of their own territories, jackals will not attack prey; birds respect the territorial rights of other birds; and apes tend to accept social hierarchies. Secured frames are honoured and modifications of rules and boundaries are rare. Why, then, are humans so fearful of secured frames and so strongly inclined towards frame modifications?

Evolution and frames

The turning point in animal responses to rules, frames, and boundaries appears to have been the acquisition of language

(Langs, 1996). This development, the most distinctive feature of our species, *Homo sapiens sapiens* (Bickerton, 1990; Corballis, 1991; Dennett, 1996; Lieberman, 1991), came about 150,000 years ago, after nearly 6 million years of hominid existence. Language was an essential factor in many unprecedented developments, including a firm sense of self and of personal and interpersonal boundaries. By means of language, humans developed a clear sense of their individual identities as distinguished from others, who were, in turn, experienced as similarly distinct persons. Language was also the basis for the ability to establish and manipulate internal representations of events and individuals, thereby freeing humans from a fixation on immediate life moments and enabling them to think about past and future events as they pleased.

Language-based intelligence has fostered many favourable hominid developments of a social and technological nature. The same capacities, however, have generated awesome realizations related to the origins and end of life—birth and death—as they apply to oneself and others. Critically, language led to the development of *existential death anxieties*, a distinctive and universal human dread.

Existential death anxiety shares the role of fundamental human anxieties with another form of death anxiety that has a much longer history than the existential form—*predatory death anxiety*. This type of anxiety exists in many non-human species, and in humans it entails the fear of death primarily from external sources such as natural disasters, assaults by conspecifics (other humans), and attacks by members of other species; assaults from within via diseases of one's own body are a mixed form—internal yet external—of this type of danger.

These two forms of death anxiety—existential and predatory—combine to create a major constellation of conscious and especially unconscious dread which is a powerful motivating force for human behaviour. These anxieties are the most fundamental factor in how humans create and respond to rules, frames, and boundaries, and they greatly influence human adaptation and maladaptations as well (Langs, 1997).

Evolving the emotion-processing mind

To understand fully the attitudes and behaviours of both patients and therapists with respect to the ground rules of psychotherapy, we must consider again nature's selection for two-system emotion-processing minds (Langs, 1996). Early hominids appear to have had single, conscious-system emotional minds that were focused on their *environments* and far less on their inner mental worlds and needs. Their minds possessed a superficial unconscious storage system, a memory reservoir that, in time, developed a filter with respect to the recall of past events and their crudely perceived meanings—an early conscious-system repressive barrier. Communication was probably direct and manifest, with a small amount of implication and of readily detected encoded meaning.

Over the period of 6 million years, selection pressures led to changes (many of which have happened relatively recently by evolutionary standards) in the design of this relatively simple cognitive module through which emotional adaptations were effected. In addition to the recent development of the awareness and anticipation of personal death, notable *selection pressures* included clan development; the need to care for newborns well into adolescence; increasing socialization and more and more complex social mores and demands, elaboration of technologies, including weapons used in warfare and other situations to harm others; and, relatively recently, the development of agriculture and settlements, which concentrated individuals in central locales.

These massive developments contributed to the escalation of emotionally charged environmental impingements to a level far beyond those with which earlier hominids had to cope. A state of mental-system emotional *overload and dysfunction* is likely to have eventuated. With individual and species survival gravely threatened, natural selection evidently opted for minds that possessed a capacity for the *unconscious perception* of selected emotionally charged meanings. This enabled humans to by-pass the conscious registration and awareness of many emotionally charged impingements and thereby reduce the intensity and burden on the conscious mind caused by distracting and disturbing emotional events and their multiple meanings. This advance led to the establishment of a second mental system that was able to process this threatening, emotionally charged, unconsciously perceived information and meaning.

The evolved architecture of the emotion-processing mind spares the conscious system from dysfunctional overloads of emotional meaning. The survival functions of the conscious system—for example, perception, reality testing, and the search for food, shelter, safety, and companionship—are thereby safeguarded. The unique, death-related selection pressures experienced by language-using hominids favoured the "choice" of those emotion-processing minds that were best able to mobilize *obliterating mental and communicative defences and knowledge reduction with respect to conscious awareness of traumatic environmental events and their meanings*.

Defence and obliteration were favoured over active conscious coping in that the resolution of these death-related anxieties was elusive, if not impossible. The need for denial mechanisms to adapt to predatory and existential death anxieties has led to a severe reduction in the understanding of emotional issues and experiences—and to a conscious preference for deviant rather than secured frames. This preference for denial-based mechanisms over direct insight means that humans know far less about their emotionally charged environments than they realize. This development also runs counter to the usual evolutionary tendency to select for capabilities that increase an organism's sensitivity to its critically relevant surroundings. The acid test of a mutation's value is the extent to which it enhances adaptation, extends personal life, and increases reproductive success. The preference for less rather than more openness and sensitivity to emotionally charged events has greatly compromised human emotional life—and psychotherapeutic pursuits as well.

The selection for enhanced defences and diminished awareness of the environment has been fateful for human emotional adaptations. By design, and reinforced by personal psychodynamic factors, humans over-use denial and repression in dealing with emotionally charged triggers—these defences are inherent to the use of unconscious perception and processing. The many death-related issues that overload the conscious mind with irresolvable dilemmas and disruptive anxieties played a major role in this preference for defence over insight.

In most individuals, the evolutionary pattern of moving towards more and more obliteration is repeated personally as death-related traumas impinge on them as the years pass. As a result, these mental defences tend to become fixed and are used repetitively. These obliterating operations take two forms (Langs, 1997):

1. *Mental defences*, which come in two varieties:
   a. *psychological*, the use of denial and repression;
   b. *communicative*, the use of disguise/encoding and non-communication.

2. *Behavioural defences*, which include acting out, mindless behavioural lapses that often have notable harmful consequences, and other actions designed primarily to discharge anxieties and pathological needs without a language-based expression of the issues involved—in essence, they are forms of blind action.

The price paid for this defensive alignment is great. With respect to adapting to emotionally charged triggering events, the conscious system is not only poorly informed, but also inclined towards actions that are harmful to oneself and others. Unconscious guilt, a major motivating force in every patient, and fears of death silently exert significant effects on the actions and thinking of the conscious mind. The greater part of emotionally relevant wisdom is located in the deep unconscious system—the conscious mind is only rarely insightful regarding critical emotional issues. The perceptions and processing activities of the deep unconscious system tend to be relatively non-defended, and its adaptive intelligence—partly inherited and partly built up unconsciously—is a great resource.

The need for conscious non-awareness is so great and the anxieties at issue so overwhelming that deep unconscious perceptions and the knowledge reflected in their processing have no means of directly entering awareness. Because of this constraint, humans are unable to utilize their greatest insights into emotional issues.

Furthermore, unconscious perceptions and experience lead to *displaced actions*—misdirected reactions and behaviours that are consciously rationalized even though their most compelling motives are unconscious. Emotionally, humans are forever reacting to the wrong person for the wrong (conscious) reasons. Emotional maladaptations and symptoms have similar sources.

Death anxiety
and the psychotherapy frame

To complete this picture, we need to understand the complex connections between rules, frames, and boundaries and the human awareness of death. Death anxiety was a *major selection* factor in the evolution of the highly defensive design of the emotion-processing mind. It also is a major psychodynamic force in the development of individual psychological and communicative defences directed against the impact of death-related traumas and the anxieties that they cause. Where, then, do rules, frames, and boundaries come into this picture?

The fundamental existential rule of life is that it ends in death. Unconsciously, then, this rule stands as the deepest or core meaning of all rules. Adhering to the ground rules of psychotherapy implicitly acknowledges and accepts this existential principle. Modifying or breaking a ground rule at bottom defies the existential rule of "life proceeds to death" and creates the unconscious illusion or delusion that the rule-breaker is an exception to that most telling certainty. Humans are therefore strongly inclined towards rule breaking.

A second link between death and the framework of psychotherapy derives from the restrictive qualities of the secured frame. The ideal ground rules of psychotherapy inherently offer maximum protection and support to both patient and therapist, but they do so by limiting the satisfactions each may obtain and by providing a restrictive set of conditions for the therapy. This sense of entrapment activates unconscious death anxieties built around the claustrum aspects of the entrapment by life that can be escaped only through death—or in illusory fashion by breaking rules.

Another connection between death and the ground rules of therapy arises from the human preference to cope with death and death anxieties primarily by means of the defence of *denial*. This mechanism may take a strictly *mental form*, as seen in a conscious denial of the inevitability of one's own death or, in extreme cases, the refusal to accept the death of someone who has actually died. But there also are *behavioural forms of denial* such as manic flights, extravagant celebrations, and excessive sexuality.

Frame modifications should now be added to this list. They may take the form of actual frame breaks in therapy or in life, but they are also an element of all frame-defying beliefs related to prior- and after-lives. *Frame modifications are a major behavioural means of denying the inevitability of personal demise. Frame-breakers unconsciously believe that they will find immortality through their frame-defying actions.*

Frame violations are, then, unconsciously sought by patients—and therapists—as ways of denying death, defending against the dread of annihilation and feelings of helplessness that they experience in the face of death, and establishing one's power over rules and restrictions. They also function as a way of shoring up defences against the expression of narratives that encode patients' telling unconscious perceptions of their therapists' death anxieties in light of their deviant framing efforts. The evolved emotion-processing mind defends itself against death anxiety most tellingly through frame modifications.

The frame and the two systems of the mind

We now have sufficient perspective to explore the links between the evolution of the two-system emotion-processing mind and human responses to rules, frames, and boundaries. The conscious system is charged with effecting direct, behavioural adaptations to environmental impingements. This system is well defended against—and therefore generally insensitive to—death-related meanings and anxieties. This necessary attitude spares the conscious mind anxieties that could interfere with its moment-to-moment efforts at coping.

While all adult humans are aware of death and of their future non-existence, these realizations are kept muted and at bay by conscious system defences such as denial and repression. If used in moderation, these defences are generally adaptive rather than maladaptive because the sceptre of personal demise is so unbearable that a measure of denial-based defence facilitates rather than interferes with emotional and general adaptational efforts.

The persistent and most intense realizations of future personal death are relegated to a subsystem of the deep unconscious system called *the fear–guilt subsystem* (Langs, 1995). The guilt function of this subsystem is based on guilt that accumulates through hurts— real and imagined—to others and self, while the fear of death materializes in infancy as soon as language and the concepts of self and future time are established. *The fear-guilt subsystem exerts powerful unconscious effects on the conscious system* and deeply affects direct actions, choices, and adaptations. Evolution has selected for this influence and has precluded effects on conscious operations by the invaluable deep unconscious wisdom subsystem.

There are at least two reasons for this unexpected choice. First, deep unconscious processing and wisdom are cognitive functions, and for them to be effective they must be articulated to a large extent through language. They therefore require a well-defined awareness of the terrifying, trigger-based experience of others and oneself that have been precluded from awareness on the perceptual level. The emotion-processing mind has been designed to screen out conscious awareness of these disturbing perceptions, and, as a result, the knowledge-base used to process them, and the results of these adaptive processing efforts, cannot enter awareness or affect conscious adaptation.

A second reason for this choice lies with the excessive human inclination towards violence against others and, less so, towards oneself. The need to control aggressive impulses is a selection pressure that favoured the influence of unconscious guilt and the fear of death through retaliation as ways of controlling these aggressive impulses. In addition, the need for denial mechanisms to deal with existential death anxieties favoured minds that unconsciously—that is, without awareness of the dread—influence the conscious system to act in ways that serve to deny death and its ultimate certainty.

Rules, frames, and boundaries create constraints that threaten humans with an inability to obtain the resources necessary for individual survival. These limitations are a common cause of conflict and violence on all levels of social interaction. Rules require the renunciation of many satisfactions and needs that humans are generally intent on gratifying, regardless of the cost. Humans insist on separateness when they long for rule-breaking mergers that will help them to deny death through magical, eternal unions with others. Thus they also insist on violating rules in order to engage in interpersonal mergers that will enable them to obliterate their separateness from others and their individual identity—much of this in the service of denying the inevitability of personal demise. Rules, frames, and boundaries also serve as reminders of one's personal limitations and mortality, and they work against the denial-based search for unlimited power and never-ending life.

Accepting a secured framework for psychotherapy asks that both patients and therapists manage and renounce many powerful but disruptive needs. It asks for thought and patience in a world where action is overvalued, and for acceptance of one's mortality, weaknesses, and vulnerabilities. The defensive protection provided by modified frames and rule breaking must also be surrendered in the service of establishing a sound holding and healing environment. With denial and blind action so strongly favoured consciously over accepting these limitations, most patients and therapists prefer frame-breaking to frame-securing—and, unawares, they pay dearly for this preference.

Given the short-term relief provided by deviant frames and the accompanying psychological denial of the price paid for this relief, few patients or therapists are inclined to invest in the long-term rewards of a secured therapy situation—no matter how great they are. Humans tend to invest far more in short-term rather than long-term results, no matter how destructive the former may be and how enhancing the latter generally are. They are also inclined to avoid dealing with secured-frame anxieties no matter how healing such therapeutic work with these issues may be.

To summarize: the development of language, which brought with it many advances in the capabilities and qualities of life of the hominid species, also brought with it an awareness of self, personal mortality, and a host of other adaptive issues virtually unknown to other species. The main effect of language acquisition on human attitudes and behaviours related to rules, frames, and boundaries was a shift from the general appreciation and honour of frames that has existed in biological species for millions of years to a deep dread of, and disrespect for, these invaluable constraints. This change in attitude has been fateful for both psychotherapy and the history of human life on this planet.

The frame positions
of two mental systems

We can now summarize and extend our understanding of the frame attitudes, needs, and preferences of the two systems of the emotion-processing mind. The *conscious system* is concerned with survival and with obliterating overly intense emotional concerns. It is designed and psychodynamically inclined towards eliminative defences in response to emotionally charged environmental impingements and strongly favours both repression and denial—beginning at the perceptual level. The conscious system is motivated towards action-discharge, gratification of pathological needs with an accompanying denial of cost, and the build-up of illusions of omnipotence and immortality.

These dominant defensive operations render the conscious system generally frame-insensitive. The conscious mind has little grasp of the nature and critical functions of rules, frames, and boundaries and seldom considers frame issues in the course of its interactions. Its focus on conflict, self, interpersonal transactions, meanings, psychodynamics, and genetics serves in this respect as defences against realizations related to the more basic and powerful realm of ground rules and settings.

In addition to being frame-insensitive, the conscious system is, in general, inclined towards modifying rather than securing frames. The system will at times favour frame-securing interventions, but this occurs mainly when frame deviations have caused extreme and unmistakable harm. Often, however, even in the face of obvious damage, the conscious system continues to accept and prefer frame deviations to secured frames. Unconsciously motivated by existential death anxieties, the conscious system is in most instances an unwitting, frame-modifying system.

In sharp contrast, *the deep unconscious system* has developed unconsciously from infancy on as an adaptive cognitive module with great sensitivity to, and appreciation for, stable and secured rules, frames, and boundaries—it is the part of the human mind that extends nature's usual view of this domain. Evidently motivated to favour the long-term needs of the individual, this system is relatively unconcerned with personal death and dedicated to adapting openly and forthrightly to unconsciously perceived meanings and their ramifications.

The deep unconscious system is relatively non-defensive in its pursuits. It seldom uses denial, which it invokes only in the face of overwhelming trauma—as seen, for example, in the initial expression of positive encoded themes following a severe physical or psychological assault. This relatively unguarded approach enables the deep unconscious system to concentrate on the status and implementation of the highly important task of pointing to the need to secure rules, frames, and boundaries regardless of the conscious anxieties that they may arouse. While the conscious mind believes that survival is enhanced mainly by frame breaking, the deep unconscious system thinks and knows the very opposite—that, in the long run, survival is favoured by frame securing. The split between the conscious and unconscious systems of the human mind is most clearly played out in their framing preferences.

Divided attitudes towards frames:
a vignette

The following brief excerpt illustrates the universal frame tendencies of the two systems of the emotion-processing mind (see also the vignette of Ms Jensen in chapter five).

Mr Rush, a married man suffering from potency problems and sudden inexplicable outbursts of rage directed most often at his wife, was in psychotherapy with Dr Burke, a woman therapist. His problems had taken a turn for the worse soon after his mother had died suddenly in an automobile accident on her way to see her physician. He blamed himself for her death because he had excused himself from driving her to the doctor and she was killed when the car she was riding in with a friend was hit by a truck that had run a red light.

A year into his therapy, Mr Rush began a session by telling Dr Burke that he'd seen a urologist because he'd developed a urinary problem. Tests revealed an infection, and he was scheduled for a cystoscopy the following week at the time of his therapy session, so he asked Dr Burke to change the time of the session. It seemed only fair to make the change; not doing so would penalize him for being ill.

Dr Burke had not established a ground rule regarding her patient's responsibility for his sessions, nor had she stated a policy regarding make-up sessions. There were, however, no other blatantly deviant aspects to the framework of the therapy—the referral had come through Mr Rush's internist, and the patient—who paid for his therapy on his own—had no outside knowledge about his therapist.

In responding to Mr Rush's request, Dr Burke indicated that she would check her schedule before the session ended to see whether she had an open hour that she could offer him. For now, she suggested that Mr Rush talk about whatever was on his mind. He responded by saying that a memory had come to mind—he had no idea why it had popped up.

He hadn't mentioned it before in his therapy, but he'd been engaged to be married soon after he quit college. His fiancée's name was Elly, and he had met her at a party given by the advertising firm that he had gone to work for after he left school. They had gone together for some months and decided to get married. He gave her a ring and they set a date, but, soon after, she became very nervous about getting married. She asked him to postpone the wedding for six months, saying that she wasn't ready to make a commitment. If he'd give her time, she was sure she could get used to the idea and allow the marriage to go forward. In the belief that her request made sense, he agreed to the delay.

Three months later, Mr Rush discovered that Elly was having an affair with another man in their office. He immediately broke off the engagement, feeling that he'd been blind to what her need to delay the marriage really meant. He commented that when you make a commitment, you should stick to it; if you don't, then something's really wrong. He never should have agreed to postpone the wedding: the delay gave her permission to wander off, and the results were disastrous. But he did learn something from what happened—he should have established a clear understanding with her as soon as they had gotten engaged, and they both should have stuck to it through thick and thin.

Consciously, Mr Rush seemed to have a good reason for asking his therapist for a frame modification. Dr Burke's failure to establish the ground rule for responsibility for sessions is a frame-modifying technical error because this aspect of the ground rules should be clearly defined for the patient in the consultation session. The secured frame calls for patients' full responsibility for all scheduled sessions and no make-up hours for missed sessions—a consistent day and a consistent time for the sessions are essential parts of the relatively fixed frame.

Through its encoded themes, the patient's material indicates that deeply unconsciously Mr Rush was quite aware of the ideal frame and knew that his request for a change in the time of his session was frame-deviant even though his therapist had never articulated this particular ground rule. The themes reflect a response to the anticipated frame-deviant trigger that says that, were Dr Burke to agree to the change, she would be violating her commitment to the patient (this adaptive assessment is encoded via the allusion to his fiancée's violation of the engagement contract). The images also imply that this act would lead to further frame breaks and would be experienced as a form of sexual disloyalty, a way of being unfaithful to him (encoded in the fiancée's affair). There also is a model of rectification, a directive to Dr Burke as to how she should manage the frame and handle Mr Rush's request: stick to the agreed upon time and don't change the time of the session (encoded in the patient's thoughts that he never should have agreed to postpone the engagement).

Based in part on in-built evolved sensitivities and in part on years of deeply unconscious experiences, the deep unconscious system has a natural, intuitive knowledge of the specific ground rules that make up the ideal framework of therapy. These unconsciously sought rules are validated through patients' derivative, encoded narratives—even when they have not been explicitly stated by the therapist. The failure of the therapist to do so is criticized unconsciously by Mr Rush—it is encoded in the comment that he should have spelled out the agreement between himself and his fiancée when they became engaged, and it should then have been stuck to through thick and thin.

The comment about not being penalized for being ill is a typical conscious system argument for frame deviations. The plea contradicts the patient's encoded images, which argue strongly against the modification. Were Dr Burke to change the time of the session, consciously the patient would be pleased. Driven, however, by his negative unconscious perceptions, he might complain about other aspects of Dr Burke's work. He would also displace his anger and feelings of betrayal onto someone in his everyday life—most probably his wife. The therapist's frame-break would provide unconscious motivations that would reinforce the very symptom that Mr Rush was hoping to resolve in his therapy.

Were the session in question and his financial responsibility for its fee maintained, Mr Rush might complain consciously. But his own encoded support for this intervention would be available to enable him to appreciate his own deep unconscious need and preference for a stable and secured frame for his therapy. Additionally, the deep unconscious experience of an actual frame-securing moment would generate positive encoded themes that, through interpretation, would enable the patient to appreciate the soundness of the therapist's frame-securing intervention and, all in all, have highly favourable therapeutic effects.

In the session, Dr Burke did not interpret her patient's encoded derivatives, which reflected his deep unconscious adaptive response to the anticipated frame break. Instead, she commented on Mr Rush's inclination to select women like his mother, who disappoint him and give him excuses to be rageful. The patient listened and said that hearing that old saw again left him cold.

He was annoyed that Dr Burke had not looked into her book for another time for next week's session and complained that she was insensitive to his needs. She reminded him of his mother, alright, but only because his mother never listened to him—she was always ranting and raving about her own problems.

Dr Burke then checked her schedule and offered an alternative hour. The patient was pleased and expressed his gratitude for his therapist's flexibility. After a brief pause, a weird magazine article he had read the other night came to Mr Rush's mind. It seemed that this woman, a nutritionist and researcher, did a study of two groups of rats. One group was fed on a strict schedule, and the other was allowed to eat whenever it liked. Oddly enough, the scheduled rats thrived, while many of the rats without a schedule overate themselves to death. People think that rats can be exploited like that—it was a terrible experiment for her to perform.

Struck by the themes in this story, Dr Burke pointed out that she had just taken Mr Rush off his schedule. She wondered if he wasn't telling her that her rescheduling his session was an over-indulgence that was very destructive to him—that in some sense, it might even kill him. Perhaps they should keep to their scheduled times for sessions so that he could flourish.

Mr Rush reacted by objecting to Dr Burke's going back on her word, but then had the odd thought that one of the ironies of his mother's death was that the truck driver who had hit the car that his mother was riding in had changed his schedule that day—he was usually in another city at the time of the accident. Maybe there is something destructive about changing things around. His father had been a stickler for keeping to commitments. He liked to tell the story of how he had once shown up on time for an appointment that the other man had forgotten. Someone else in the firm that he was visiting agreed to see him, and, after they had talked, the man offered his father a job in the firm—it was a major advance for his father.

Dr Burke pointed to the encoded message in this last story—

that keeping appointments was well rewarded—and said that she would hold Mr Rush to the usual time of his session and ask him to be responsible for the fee for it. She also indicated that she would adopt that as her policy—that the time of his sessions would be fixed—and she asked that he accept financial responsibility for all of his scheduled hours. Mr Rush then smiled and said that he now realized that it would be easy for him to change the day of his cystoscopy. He wondered why he hadn't thought of that before. His thoughts next turned to his mother's being pinned in the car and crushed to death. Since the session was nearly over, Dr Burke pointed out that with the ground rule for the time of his sessions fixed, he seemed to feel trapped and to have images related to being killed. She then said that time was up, and the session ended.

This additional segment of the vignette demonstrates a series of typical responses to both modifying and securing the ground rules of therapy. When Dr Burke did not decode her patient's encoded messages and secure the frame as his derivatives suggested, Mr Rush became angry. Manifestly, he was annoyed about not getting his hour changed, but the deep unconscious source of the anger was his therapist's missed interpretation and failure to secure the frame. Here, too, the attitudes of the two systems of the emotion-processing mind stand at opposite poles—the conscious source of anger is the exact opposite of its deep unconscious source.

This formulation is supported by the patient's response once the therapist offered the alternative session. The encoded themes clearly pointed to the destructiveness of the proposed frame break and portray the persecutory, predatory death anxieties that are always evoked when a ground rule of therapy is modified—or about to be altered. This encoded image was sufficiently clear and strong for Dr Burke to hear and decode it, and to link it to its trigger—her planned change in the time of the following hour. These realizations led her to interpret the themes in light of the intended frame change and to move towards securing the frame. These interventions obtained encoded validation in the stories about the cause of the death of his mother, which involved a frame change, and about the rewards reaped by Mr Rush's frame-securing father. There then followed an image that reflects the emergence of the patient's secured-frame, entrapment, existential death anxieties—encoded in the image of the patient's mother trapped in the car.

This is a typical psychotherapy sequence, with conscious pleas for a frame modification accompanied by a continual flow of encoded images that speak against the change. The exact meanings of the modified and secured frames will have a personal cast, but the general themes are always the same. Whereas the conscious mind is inconsistent and adopts varied frame-related attitudes in different individuals, the deep unconscious system is extremely consistent.

The key unconscious issues for Mr Rush at the time involved the conflicts, guilt, and death anxiety created by the death of his mother. In seeking to change the time of his session, unconsciously he was endeavoring to punish and harm himself, as his mother had been harmed. This unconscious wish is reflected in the story of the death of the rats that overfed through self-indulgence. He was also trying to deny his own vulnerability to death by showing that he had the power to change and defy the ground rules of his therapy. But once the frame was secured, his deep unconscious experience shifted to a positive introject of his therapist and then an identification with his mother and to entrapment anxieties and existential death anxieties.

Death anxiety is a continuous issue for patients and therapists. When the frame is modified, the death anxiety becomes predatory; when it is secured, it is existential. However, there are crucial differences in these two forms of frame-evoked death anxiety. The predatory death anxieties are based on a true experience of being harmed and exploited—in Mr Rush's words, being subjected to a terrible experiment. Mistrust and danger prevail, and communicating meaningfully—be it consciously or unconsciously—is dangerous:the therapy is compromised, and harm is done to the patient.

In contrast, the existential death anxieties evoked by secured-frame conditions are an inevitable part of life. Secured frames are not predatory: they do not entail harmful actions by the therapist.

These frames offer inherent support, holding, and safety, attributes that not only help patients emotionally, but also provide a safe set of conditions for open and powerful communication—and insight—on all levels. Secured frames offer the ideal conditions for dealing adaptively with life's emotional stresses, amongst which the inevitability of personal death looms large.

PART TWO

THE SPECIFIC GROUND RULES

CHAPTER SEVEN

The secured setting
in private practice

A s is true in life itself, frame issues are a never-ending feature of a psychotherapy experience. At all times, ground rules are being held secured or rectified on the one hand, or sustained as deviant or actively being modified on the other. As a therapy unfolds, the frame is at all times in a particular state or being actively managed and responded to by both patient and therapist.

Many clinical issues arise in connection with dealing with the setting and the various ground rules of psychotherapy. We therefore turn now to a detailed examination of these canons in order to understand what each contributes to the secured frame and the effects of its modification. Clinical precepts are developed with regard to frame-related intervening in and solving of frame problems as they arise in both private practice and clinic settings. Both frame-management and frame-related interpreting are explored. I begin with the components of the *relatively fixed frame*, turning first to the setting of private psychotherapy.

The main elements of the setting

The setting of psychotherapy is the basic physical–structural context of the treatment experience. Although the setting is inanimate and usually relatively unchanging, its form and management conveys a great deal about the therapist as perceived by the patient consciously and especially unconsciously. One of the most fundamental frame statements made by a therapist is expressed in the offer of a setting for psychotherapy. An ideal setting speaks for a basic frame-securing approach to adapting, interacting, and doing therapy, while a compromised setting speaks for frame-deviant qualities to these efforts. The deep unconscious system is extremely sensitive to the implications of this aspect of the treatment situation.

In general, therapists who offer secured settings tend to secure the other ground rules of therapy. Specific exceptions to this rule are, however, not uncommon—perhaps the most frequent being third-party fee coverage for a therapy that nevertheless takes place in a secured setting. On the other hand, therapists who employ modified settings almost always alter other basic ground rules. Most often these entail violations of total privacy and confidentiality—for example, home-office arrangements and shared waiting-rooms. Furthermore, the setting may be private and closed and thereby speak for safety, or open and quasi-public and therefore unsafe. For example, a waiting-room that is shared with other therapists exposes the patient to the therapist's office-mates and their patients, and a home-office exposes the patient to family members and vice versa.

The following are the important features of the psychotherapy setting, listed with the ideal frame and most disruptive deviations noted after each item:

1. *The location of the office*
   - Most ideal—a professional building located some distance from where the therapist lives.
   - Most disruptive—an office located in the therapist's dwelling.

   Comment: The impact of compromised locations is seldom revealed consciously by patients, but the deep unconscious response, and the behavioural and symptomatic effects, are considerable. Buildings with doormen or those in which a patient must register or be announced before entering the therapist's office are severely compromised. Most of these deviations introduce third parties into the therapy.

2. *Who uses the office*
    • Most ideal—exclusive use by the therapist.
    • Most disruptive—sharing the office with any one else during the therapist's office hours or the office being used by others when the therapist is not in there.

    Comment: The violations of total privacy and confidentiality that are built into shared office arrangements render the therapeutic space unsafe for patients. In addition, the therapist does not have full control of shared office spaces: other therapists and their patients often intrude into a therapy in ways that adversely impacts on the patient's therapeutic experience.

3. *The status of the waiting-room*
    • Most ideal—a private waiting-room.
    • Most disruptive—sharing a waiting-room with other therapists or anyone else.

    Comment: See point 2, above.

4. *The bathroom arrangements*
    • Most ideal—separate bathrooms for the therapist and his or her patients. A suitable alternative is a single, in-office bathroom, preferably one that the therapist can reach without going through the waiting-room and that the patient can access without intruding on another patient's session.
    • Most disruptive—a public-access bathroom in the hall of an office building, or the patient's use of a therapist's bathroom within his or her abode.

    Comment: It is especially important to avoid bathroom arrangements that make it possible for a patient and therapist to meet in the lavatory; such a meeting entails a severely seductive and assaultive frame break. The use of a therapist's personal bathroom is similarly seductive and self-revealing.

5. *The soundproofing*

    *   Most ideal—a completely soundproofed consultation-room.
    *   Most disruptive—any sound leakage whatsoever, especially if words being spoken within the consultation-room can be heard in the waiting-room and/or if words from the outside can penetrate into the consultation-room.

    Comment: The emission of sounds from, or the entry of sounds into, the consultation-room renders the space open to the public. This greatly harms the patient and compromises the meaning aspects of the patient's manifest and encoded communications—to the detriment of the therapy. While conscious avoidance of mentioning this type of frame break is typical, patients will on occasion comment manifestly on hearing people speaking in the hallway or waiting-room of a therapist's office. In both types of situations—that is, with or without a direct allusion by the patient to the frame break—it is crucial for the therapist to allow the patient an opportunity to tell stories. These narratives encode the patient's deep unconscious experience and assessment of this kind of frame modification.

6. *The nature of the decor and appointments of the space*

    *   Most ideal—a simple decor that is minimally revealing personally for the therapist.
    *   Most disruptive—the exposure of personal photographs, *objets d'art*, and anything else that unnecessarily reveals something personal about the therapist.

7. *Reading material in the waiting-room*

    *   Most ideal—the absence of any kind of reading material.
    *   Most disruptive—the presence of magazines, books, or pamphlets, because they reveal something personal about the therapist.

    Comment: Magazines are violations of the therapist's relative anonymity in that the therapist's choices are unnecessarily self-revealing. The waiting-room is a space for a patient's contemplations and should be without distractions or self-revelations from the therapist. In addition, reading materials unconsciously invite patients either to ask their therapists for permission to borrow a book or magazine, or covertly to take one or the other on leaving the office.

8. *Telephone arrangements*
    • Ideal—an answering machine that is placed out of sight, and, if possible, a telephone that is also located out of sight. In addition, the telephone should be turned off and not answered during sessions.
    • Most disruptive—A telephone on the therapist's desk that he or she answers during sessions. Also, the use of an answering service, which introduces third parties and sources of error and deviations into a therapy.
    Comment: The essential needs here are for a silent telephone and answering machine—a noisy one brings the intrusion of a third party into the patient's session—and for the therapist to refrain from answering the telephone during a session. Telephone-answering services are likely to be unreliable, and they break the frame by involving third parties in patients' therapies.

The setting is the consistent and reliable backdrop or stage for the unfolding of the therapy. It is an essential part of the therapist's hold and containment of, and adaptation to, the patient. The setting reflects the extent of the therapist's consistency and stability, and his or her preferred means of coping with adaptation-evoking, emotionally charged triggering events.

In all, then, selecting an office space in which to do psychotherapy is a critical decision, with abundant conscious and deep unconscious meanings and consequences. However consciously rationalized or necessary, the selection of a basically deviant setting speaks strongly for a therapist's frame-modifying needs and mode of adaptation—and all that these imply.

The ideal setting

To summarize, the *unconsciously validated*, ideal setting for a psychotherapy experience entails a location in a professional building at some distance from the therapist's residence—if possible, each should be located in a different town or section of a city. The office door has a room number, but possibly no nameplate. The office is used exclusively by a single therapist, and the waiting-room is private and not used by anyone else, professional or otherwise, even when the therapist is not in the office. It is plainly but tastefully furnished with simple appointments.

There are separate bathrooms for patients and the therapist, or a single bathroom within the office that is easily accessed by all concerned. The consultation-room is fully soundproofed and, if possible, has its own exit, which allows the patient to leave the office without returning to the waiting-room. In the consultation-room, there are coat hooks or a coat rack on which a patient can hang his or her coat or a chair on which it can be placed. There is also a closet, whose door is kept closed, in which the therapist can hang his or her coat and store necessary supplies and a silently operating answering machine—the telephone is turned off during sessions. The windows are covered and there is no view to the outside—a closed space is vital for the necessary sense of privacy and confidentiality of the secured frame.

There is a single setting in which a given patient is seen, even when a therapist has two offices (in which case, information about the second office is not shared with the patient). The therapist should have a desk, with a chair for the patient in front of it or to the side, for seeing patients face-to-face. An acceptable alternative is a setting without a desk, but with two facing chairs, one for the patient and the other for the therapist—with a table between the chairs if possible. In addition, for therapists so inclined, there should be a couch for the patient to lie on and a chair for the therapist to sit on, set behind the couch so that the therapist cannot be seen by the patient when he or she is on the couch. A small table set between the chair and the couch is a useful physical boundary.

* * *

This recitation of the ideal setting may strike the reader as an expression of Puritanism, but this is not the case. The deep unconscious system of the mind of every patient and therapist is unswerving in its commitment to an ideal, secured frame for psychotherapy—and for their personal lives as well. Thus, the rarity of settings of this kind and the general lack of appreciation for their necessity reflects the failure of therapists to decode their patient's narrative themes consistently in light of frame-related triggering interventions. Buttressed by the denial of the detrimental consequences of deviant settings, the natural conscious preference for deviant frames causes considerable harm to both patients and therapists. Secured settings are the foundation for secured and deeply successful therapy experiences.

CHAPTER EIGHT

Deviant settings
in private practice

The ideal private setting is a rarity. The conscious system invents countless rationalizations to justify the unconsciously driven need for deviant frames and settings—much of it stemming from the influence of the deep unconscious fear–guilt subsystem on the conscious mind. For example, economic pressures are used to justify therapists' decisions to share waiting-rooms, have their offices where they live, or rent office space to or from others. But these conscious needs are strongly driven by deep unconscious motives in therapists that prompt them to establish deviant settings as part of their way of adapting to their own emotional issues. The common unconscious motives involved in this trend include an unrecognized dread of secured settings, unresolved existential death anxieties, and fears of the deep unconscious meanings that materialize within secured frames—many of them involving patients' unconscious perceptions of therapists' emotional dysfunctions as reflected in both their choice of deviant settings and other non-validated interventions.

The home-office and the shared waiting-room are among the most frequently used compromised settings. I turn now for a closer look at each of these deviant settings.

The home-office

The home-office, whether an apartment or house, located within the therapist's living quarters or separate from them, modifies the relative anonymity of the therapist and exposes his or her patients to family members—and the reverse. As a self-disclosure and breach of the total privacy and confidentiality of the therapy, this frame break creates a social and non-professional cast to the treatment.

This kind of frame modification is termed a *vested-interest deviation* (Langs, 1979), because the therapist modifies the frame largely for personal reasons in disregard for the therapeutic needs of his or her patients. This kind of frame modification is both seductive and destructive, and it functions for both patients and therapists as a maladaptive defence against separation, loss, and death anxiety. There is no sound reason for a therapist to use this kind of setting for his or her therapeutic work.

Vested-interest deviations are difficult to explore and even more difficult to resolve. Often, therapists naively follow their teachers or own therapists in making this choice of setting. The therapist who is committed to the deviation is also likely to become *derivative-deaf* with respect to patients' encoded themes related to the deviant setting—their frame-related meanings will repeatedly be missed (Langs, 1982, 1992). Furthermore, patients tend unconsciously to protect their therapists from conscious guilt and conflict by avoiding this subject both manifestly and in their encoded narratives. This enables therapists who work in these deviant settings to continue to do so for long periods of time, seldom consciously aware of the damage that the setting is causing to their patients—and to themselves via the unconscious guilt that the hurtful aspects of the deviation evokes in them.

Typically, patients will not mention the modified setting even when there is an acute, frame-deviant incident, as, for example, when a patient sees or even talks to a therapist's spouse or child. Most patients unconsciously restrict themselves to encoding a bridging and power theme or two in response to such incidents. These themes are easily missed by the therapist, in part because he or she is unaware of the acute triggering incident.

As a rule, the only time that these issues materialize with any consistency and in workable form is when a therapist decides to leave the home-office for a private, professional space. At such times, prior blatant incidents with family members and others are suddenly recalled by patients, and the unconscious meanings of these experiences finally appear in patients' encoded themes in a manner that allows them to be linked to past and present triggers—and interpreted.

Because these settings unconsciously promote strong communicative defences that render many acute triggering events hidden from view and from therapeutic working through, these office arrangements are best avoided. The harm that they cause through negative introjects of the therapist's unconscious anxieties and deviant modes of adaptation are such that the money a therapist saves in this way is poor compensation for the damage that they cause.

Mrs Jenkins was in therapy with Dr Hart, whose office was attached to his house. The patient began a session by mentioning that as she came in she had seen a woman leaving the house, and she was pretty sure that it was Dr Hart's wife. Her subsequent associations centred around her mistrust of men. She works with a married man, Jordan, whom everyone likes, but she's certain he cheats the company on his commissions. He also lies a lot—she can't trust anything he says. She'd like to tell her boss about Jordan's dishonesty, but she thinks the boss may be involved in the cheating, and she's convinced that if she speaks up, she'll be the one to get hurt, not Jordan.

Dr Hart pointed out that Mrs Jenkins had started the session by alluding to having seen his wife leave the house, and that she went on to speak of a man who is dishonest and whom she mistrusts. He is someone she would like to report to her boss, but she is afraid she will be hurt if she does. To connect these themes to the incident that just happened, it seems that seeing his wife has led Mrs Jenkins to mistrust him and view him as a cheater and as being dishonest. It also has made her fearful of bringing up the problem because she expects to be attacked for doing so.

Mrs Jenkins responded by saying that she couldn't see the connections Dr Hart was making—she just thought his wife
looked attractive, but a bit frazzled. She then ruminated about
the kind of husband Dr Hart must be—distractible, but nice.

The patient began the next session with a dream. She is in her
living room at home when she hears a noise in her bedroom.
She goes to the room and is shocked to find her husband in bed
with another woman. She starts screaming at them for what
they're doing—and in her own bed, no less. There was more to
the dream, but she lost it.

The main association was to her co-worker Jordan whom she
overheard talking to one of the other men at work. It seems
that Jordan had been having an affair with a woman at work,
and they were seen in a restaurant by a girlfriend of his wife.
When Jordan's wife confronted him, he at first denied any
involvement with the woman, but ended up confessing to the
affair and trying to downplay the problem. No wonder Mrs
Jenkins doesn't trust men—her own husband included.

As the session unfolded, there was no direct allusion to the
therapist, the home-office setting, or the patient's having seen
the therapist's wife. Dr Hart tried to link this dream and associations to the fact that the patient had seen his wife prior to
the previous session. But, once again, Mrs Jenkins could not
accept the connection: she thought of it as an idea in her therapist's mind, not hers. Subsequent associations were to opinion-
ated people who impose their ideas on others before they are
ready to absorb them.

This modification of the therapist's relative anonymity through
the exposure of his wife and patient to each other stems from the
frame-deviant setting. It is a kind of self-disclosure that happens
frequently under these conditions. In the session after the deviation occurred, Mrs Jenkins mentioned it directly; this is an unusual
manifest representation of this frame-deviant, adaptation-evoking
trigger.

Despite her uncommon direct reference to the frame modification, in her session Mrs Jenkins consciously shrugged off the

deviation as if it were inconsequential. In addition, her encoded narrative imagery revealed little of her deep unconscious experience of the frame break. The main themes were those of cheating and lying, and a fear of revealing herself. Evidently, she was keeping her deep unconscious experience and processing of this incident a secret from both herself and her therapist.

While Dr Hart's intervention is an effort to trigger decode the themes in light of the frame-deviant event, there are problems with what he said. For one, Dr Hart erred in the way he alluded to his wife. Once a therapist's mind has established a deviant-frame mode of adaptation, it is extremely difficult for him or her to avoid adding further frame breaks to the already deviant therapeutic conditions. The fact that Dr Hart alluded to the woman Mrs Jenkins saw as "his wife" is a technical error—a self-revelation. The proper allusion should have been to "the woman you believe to be my wife," said in a way that neither denies nor affirms the patient's impression. Except for instances where the identity of a third party has been established beyond a doubt, this is the best available technical approach to this matter.

The second problem with the intervention is that it did not include an offer of rectification. None was modelled in the patient's material, nor did Dr Hart have any intention of moving his office. Without the promise of rectification, encoded validation is rare even when an intervention appears to be relatively correct. This is one reason that working in deviant settings is more difficult for therapists—and their patients—than working in secured ones. In the absence of deep unconscious recommendations of correctives, effective therapeutic work and validating images are quite rare under frame-modified conditions.

The patient's main *communicative resistance* in the first session is typical of these deviant settings. It involves her failure to produce clear and strong encoded themes for linking to the consciously identified trigger. In the second hour, however, Mrs Jenkins showed another frequent communicative resistance seen under these circumstances. She shifted to producing strong derivatives, but without a manifest allusion to the trigger. She also did not provide a general bridge to therapy, a link that is needed for a sound playback of derivatives organized around an unmentioned frame-related trigger. Without a clear bridging image, the therapist has no effective means with which to connect the encoded themes to himself and the therapy situation.

Dr Hart tried to by-pass this resistance by introducing the missing trigger himself. He did not, however, obtain encoded validation. Instead, the derivatives were directed at the bullying quality of his trying to force his way past the patient's resistances and introduce the trigger into the manifest dialogue, rather than allowing the patient to do so herself—either manifestly or in encoded form—when she was again ready to do so.

In essence, all that Dr Hart could do was to wait for the rare session in which the patient would unconsciously elect to allude manifestly to an immediate deviation related to the setting and also generate narratives with meaningful power themes—and possibly a model of rectification as well. This diminution of communicative resistances would facilitate a full and effective interpretation of the patient's deep unconscious experience of the deviant setting. There would be a degree of therapeutic gain for the patient even in the absence of rectification of the deviant conditions by the therapist—that is, the move to a private office. But without this corrective, the patient would be likely to become disillusioned and quickly reinstate her communicative resistances—patients unconsciously know that there is no greater mode of healing than securing a deviant aspect of the framework of a therapy.

Modified therapy situations cause patients to mistrust their therapists. Patients are then unwittingly reluctant to communicate the derivatives that express their mistrust and their deep unconscious experiences of harm caused when new frame deviations arise. In these situations, patients also know that their therapists are not likely to secure the frame, and so, unconsciously, they are convinced that it is useless and dangerous to reveal their painful unconscious perceptions of the therapist in light of the existing frame modifications. In addition, patients who accept these deviant settings collaborate to fashion an unconscious, *frame-deviant misalliance* with their therapists. Strong needs for deviant frames motivate both parties to sustain the frame-altered situation. The patient generally avoids communicating powerful and bridging encoded themes and the therapist resists decoding the derivative themes that do emerge because these would lead to a conscious recognition of the need to secure the deviant setting—most often through a decision by the therapist to move his or her office space to a professional building.

Shared waiting-rooms

Similar issues are raised by shared waiting-rooms. This deviation exposes patients to other therapists and their patients. It also creates an increased vulnerability to a patient's meeting someone he or she knows—a frame-breaking exposure to a third party, with many devastating conscious and unconscious repercussions. Other problems include the inadvertent locking of the office by another therapist before the patient's session has ended, frame-violating discussions between office staff that are seen or overheard by a patient, and interruptions of sessions by confused others over whom the patient's therapist has no control.

This deviation, which is consciously motivated largely for economic reasons, also supports maladaptive defences in therapists directed against being alone with patients and against issues of loss, separation, and death. Patients unconsciously perceive these vulnerabilities in their therapists and will either be derivatively silent about them and exploit them for their own maladaptive defensive needs, or on occasion encode their deep unconscious experience of the meanings of the frame break. When these themes go uninterpreted, patients usually give up on encoded communication for long periods of time.

Deeply insightful cures are very rare if not impossible under these conditions. For any healing to occur for a patient, it would require a frame-breaking therapist who is nevertheless painfully aware of the consequences of the frame-deviant setting. This therapist would also need to be capable of interpreting his or her patients' negative deep unconscious perceptions of the damage being done by the deviant setting and able to link the exacerbations of the patient's resistances and symptoms to the modified frame. In essence, this is tantamount to the therapist's openly acknowledging that he or she is knowingly harming the patient. Furthermore, an untoward acute, frame-deviant event, such as a patient meeting a friend in the waiting-room, would virtually preclude the success of even the most skilful interpretive efforts by the therapist.

The contradictions experienced unconsciously by the patient between what the therapist says and what he or she does frame-wise would be crazy-making, while the conscious and deep unconscious guilt experienced by the therapist would have similar consequences for him or her. The pressures from the patient, on the deep unconscious level, and within the therapist, both con-sciously and deeply unconsciously, to rectify the frame would be so intense that relief for both patient and therapist could come only through frame rectification—the therapist's moving his or her practice to an entirely private office. Only those therapists who are derivative-deaf can sustain a deviation of this kind.

Finally, one other variation on frame-deviant settings deserves mention. Some therapists do not have a waiting-room in their of-fice. This missing element of the setting creates many awkward, frame-modifying moments. For example, patients must wait for their sessions in the hall or elsewhere outside the therapist's office, leaving them exposed to third parties. Under these conditions, there are also frequent errors regarding the time at which the sessions begin. Clearly, this too is a harmful departure from the ideal frame and should be avoided.

Issues of technique

Activating latent setting issues

Every aspect of a modified setting will evoke responses from a patient's deep unconscious system. However, vested-interest frame modifications that are part of the established conditions of a therapy tend to be accepted without much notice consciously— and even deep unconsciously for long periods of time. They will, however, tend to be actively addressed by the patient uncon-sciously via the expression of encoded derivatives mainly when:

1. *An active adaptation-evoking issue arises in connection with the deviant aspect of the setting.* Examples are a patient seeing a

therapist in an office hallway or a public bathroom; a friend of a patient showing up to see another therapist who shares the waiting-room with the therapist; and, in a home-office setting, someone in the therapist's family being seen by the patient.

2. *There is a frame break related to any other ground rule of the therapy.* An immediate frame modification will, as a rule, activate past frame modifications and intensify deep unconscious responses to the basic deviant conditions of a therapy.

Potential for therapeutic gain

Paradoxically, frame-deviant moments, however harmful, are also therapeutic opportunities for the patient. The patient will often reveal material and conflicts that have not been represented before—themes and unconscious experiences that have been activated by the particular nature of the frame break. The therapist may also learn a great deal about long-standing frame issues that have been lying dormant and have gone unrecognized, even as they serve as unconscious factors in stalemated therapy situations. These activated communications allow for these issues and themes to be understood and interpreted; at times, an unnoticed frame break may be rectified—a most salutary event in a therapy.

Some clinical precepts

Several basic principles of technique are useful in dealing with these deviant-setting issues.

1. A fundamental goal of the therapist should be to meet, as much as possible, the secured-frame needs of his or her patients.

2. Moments of acute frame modification require that the therapist use the active triggering event to organize the patient's story material and interpret the themes accordingly.

3. On those occasions when the frame-deviant setting is mentioned directly by the patient—for example, when a patient refers to seeing another doctor in a shared waiting-room—the

narrative material should be organized around the manifestly represented deviation. The thematic images are formulated as personally selected, valid unconscious perceptions of the meanings of the modified setting element. Even when rectification is not possible and the themes are weak, interpretation is always called for under these communicative conditions: the manifestly represented trigger is used to organize the narrative material and the interpretation is made on that basis.

Most often, the patient's images and themes will include encoded instructions to rectify the frame deviation, and the therapist should decode and interpret this directive to the patient. Wherever possible, rectification and frame securing should follow. When these efforts are soundly carried out, the patient will respond with encoded validation—for example, narratives that refer to bright and effective individuals or that extend the therapist's interpretation.

When rectification is not possible or is not carried out, the patient's response will be mixed: a small measure of encoded validation will be followed, as a rule, by encoded disappointment and anger towards a therapist who has understood the frame-deviant problem but has failed to act to correct it. Unconsciously, the contradiction within the therapist between understanding and behaviour drives the patient crazy and creates very frustrating and painful moments for the patient and therapist so involved.

4. A common sequence is one in which a deviant setting is acutely modified and the patient makes no manifest reference to the frame-deviant trigger. The therapist must therefore listen carefully for derivative themes that represent and are readily connected to the immediate frame break. A strong bridging theme that encodes the nature of the frame break, associated with a general allusion to the therapy or therapist, allows for a playback of the encoded material. When properly done, this intervention may prompt the patient's direct recall of the missing trigger and facilitate a more complete interpretation and frame-rectifying effort when possible.

It is important for a therapist to be on the alert for relevant, frame-deviant encoded themes. For example, home-office settings should lead the therapist to be watchful for stories about contaminated or inappropriate settings such as strange structures, buildings, and offices that are used for mixed or peculiar purposes, and places of ill-repute or where something dishonest is going on. Shared waiting-rooms should prompt a sensitivity to themes of exposure, run-ins with third parties, fears of being alone, and the like. Under these conditions, a "third ear" of this kind is a great asset for the therapist.

5.   When a private therapist is able to secure one or another aspect of a deviant setting, the patient is afforded a critical *healing secured-frame moment* and an opportunity for meaningful deep unconscious communication related to critical deep unconscious conflicts and issues. The patient also benefits from a favourable unconscious introject of the frame securing therapist. It also is a special occasion in which the patient can encode and then consciously experience and work through his or her fundamental existential death anxieties.

Every patient should have a chance to experience frame-securing moments if his or her cure is to be deep, lasting, and truly adaptive, and, once an aspect of the ground rules has been secured, it should stay secured. Shifting back and forth from frame modifying to frame securing tends to confuse and alienate patients and to evoke symptomatic disturbances.

In the rare therapy that is entirely secured at the outset with respect to the setting and remainder of the ground rules, the holding properties of the frame will account for much of the cure. Secured-frame anxieties will be prominent and the existential death anxieties can be interpreted in the context of the secure qualities of the framework of the therapy. In addition, momentary frame-breaking lapses by the therapist are almost inevitable, and they create opportunities to interpret the patient's unconscious perceptions of these incidents and their genetic connections. When the frame is re-secured, secured-frame themes and anxieties will re-emerge and be available for interpretation.

6.   When a private therapist works in a basically frame-modified setting, he or she will, defensively, inevitably be insensitive to

encoded themes that reflect the nature and unconscious meanings of the deviation. It therefore behoves such a therapist to develop a clear and usable picture of the universal meanings of each aspect of the setting—and of each of the ground rules of psychotherapy. Mastery of this thesaurus will automatically alert the therapist to themes that are likely to allude to an unnoticed frame modification.

For example, a meeting between a female patient and female therapist in a ladies room located outside a therapist's office will modify the ground rule pertaining to confining the locale of contact between patient and therapist to the therapist's office. There also are both a sense of self-revelation and the inappropriate exposure of both parties to each other. Themes of exhibitionism, voyeurism, homosexuality, intrusion, and such are bound to appear in the patient's subsequent encoded narratives. In a different vein, a run-in between a patient and his therapist's son in the context of a home-office setting will modify the total privacy and confidentiality of the patient's therapy and evoke themes of intruders, uninvited third parties, child molestation, seduction, and the like.

While each patient will selectively perceive those meanings of a frame break that are most relevant to his or her life history and emotional illness, the selection will be made from a group of universal properties that accrue to a given type of frame modification in keeping with its specific nature. In all cases, however, the departure from the ideal frame is experienced deep unconsciously as damaging—the nature of the harm depending on the frame break itself and the patient's prior life experiences.

Securing a deviant setting

A very special and powerful intervention by the private therapist who is working in a deviant setting—mainly a home-office or a shared waiting-room—is the move of his or her practice to a private office that is fully secured with regard to the setting and possibly in other ways as well. These moments are highly salutary for both the patients and the therapist involved, and they significantly alter the nature of the patient's conscious and unconscious experience of the therapy and therapist. They also dramatically change what the patient communicates to the therapist and how the patient generally behaves with respect to the ground rules of the therapy—and of his or her life as well. This is the kind of frame change in psychotherapy that strikingly reveals the profound influence of rules, frames, and boundaries on the therapeutic interaction and process of cure.

Technically, a therapist should decide to move to a private space on his or her own, without any manifest involvement of his or her patients—even though they will repetitively encode directives of that very kind. The new office should be available on the date that the therapist intends to begin to practice there. Patients should be notified of the pending move at least one month in advance, and, once announced, this frame-related intervention should be taken as a prime adaptation-evoking, anticipated triggering event for the patient (and, of course, the therapist as well). The therapist should therefore be alert to the unconscious implications of the move and be prepared to hear the thematic material in those terms—as well as simultaneously keeping an open mind for both unexpected derivative themes and reactions to other frame-related triggers that become activated while the move is being worked over.

This particular trigger is a classic example of interventions that involve *modifying the frame to secure it*. It is both healing and anxiety-provoking because the effects of both the existing deviant setting and the anticipated secured-frame setting are experienced and worked over deeply unconsciously—both predatory and existential death anxieties are activated and need to be resolved insightfully.

Under these conditions, both patient and therapist often experience an impulse to modify the frame in some other way—an inclination that is aroused by the unconscious need to defend against the dreaded existential death anxieties mobilized by the frame-securing change in the conditions of the treatment. Patients who accept deviant conditions for psychotherapy or counselling are strongly invested in sustaining the maladaptive protection afforded by the altered frame. They are quite terrified of the secured frame and its deep unconscious implications and especially vulnerable to the anxieties aroused when the framework for their therapies is secured. Often, similar issues exist for the frame-securing psychotherapist. It is therefore crucial for a therapist to be alerted to these issues so that he or she can safeguard these frame-securing efforts without sabotaging them in any way.

When this type of move is announced to a patient, the therapist should provide the specific date of the change-over. The address and telephone number should be mentioned, and an exception to the rule of non-recording may be necessary—the patient may have to, on his or her own, record the new address and telephone number. There should be no description of the new conditions under which the patient will be seen—this should be left to the patient's imagination and, after the move is made, to his or her conscious and unconscious experience.

The move itself should be made over a weekend so that the patients have a clear time interval between visits to the two different offices. The furniture should remain the same as much as possible, although changes of furniture, if made, are not as significant as the move itself.

The material from the patient will reflect his or her conscious and deep unconscious experience of the frame change. In general, the conscious reaction is limited to relatively minor issues—the convenience or inconvenience of the new location, the view that it is a move upwards or the reverse, and curiosity about the new locale. The deep unconscious reaction is, however, far more pervasive and sensitive. Both the deviant and frame-securing aspects will be processed and the results reflected in the patient's encoded themes. The frame-securing qualities will, with few exceptions, take precedence and arouse greater anxieties than the frame-deviant aspects. Indeed, secured-frame anxiety is the most disruptive and dreaded form of anxiety experienced by humans—patients and therapists alike. Nevertheless, these anxieties will not be fully activated until the patient is in the new, private office.

The following are some key points to keep in mind:

1. Patients who accept therapy with private therapists in frame-deviant settings have an unconscious need for modified frames. Often, they suffer from significant amounts of unresolved death anxiety, usually of the existential kind, created by severe

death-related life traumas. Unconsciously, they elect for frame modifications as a denial-based defence against these death anxieties, which would be aroused in a secured frame. They therefore become quite anxious unconsciously when a change of office is announced, because the new address usually suggests a more secured setting, particularly when the change is from a home-office to a professional building.

The least clue of a securing of the frame will activate the secured-frame death anxieties of the patient. Similarly, the moment that a therapist decides to move from a deviant to a secured setting, his or her own secured-frame anxieties will be activated, providing a special opportunity to explore and discover the basis for his or her own inevitable issues in this regard. This is best done by engaging in self-processing (Langs, 1993) in order to trace their roots and resolve the conflicts and symptoms that they have created—including unconscious needs to work in a deviant-frame setting.

2. The deep unconscious meanings of a move of this kind involve experiencing both the frame-modifying and frame-securing aspects of the move. On the frame-altering side, the move is unconsciously processed as an abandonment and as the loss and death of the therapist, who exists only in one particular space. While the conscious mind realizes that a therapist is the same person in both settings, deep unconscious experience is such that the therapist is perceived as part of the setting—as one person in the original office and quite another in the new office.

The deviant aspects of the move are also unconsciously experienced as a relatively benign betrayal of, and act of violence against, the patient, and the invitation to continue the therapy in the new office is seen as a sexual seduction. Predatory death anxieties are quite strong, but they are eminently workable because the traumatic qualities of the move—and the genetic connections—will be alluded to manifestly and meaningful power themes will appear in the patient's narrative material, especially when he or she is seen in the new office. These themes need to be interpreted via trigger decoding and linked to the deviant aspects of the move.

3. On the frame-securing side, the deep unconscious experience and themes will centre on the highly constructive sense of safety and holding that the patient is being afforded in the new

location. There also will be themes and issues of entrapment and death. The inevitability of death as a consequence of life finds its parallel expression in the experience of a health-giving secured frame, which is, as well, a space that a patient enters with the unconscious expectation that he or she will be entrapped and annihilated. In order to turn this event into a strongly therapeutic experience for the patient, this material needs to be interpreted and linked to earlier, traumatic genetic experiences. In addition, the remainder of the frame should be held secure. A positive outcome can be assured only if the therapist resolves his or her own existential death anxieties when they are activated in the new, secured setting.

4. Many deliberate and inadvertently maintained secrets— conscious and unconscious—involving the prior deviant setting are revealed once a patient is in the new, secured setting with the therapist. Incidents with office staff and other patients that occurred in a shared waiting-room and with family members at home-office arrangements typically go unreported until the office move has been made. Sexual involvements between patients who had met in shared waiting-rooms and many other kinds of deviant experiences find their way into the patient's manifest and encoded material once the secured frame has been established.

These important prior events should not, however, simply be taken at face value. They should also be understood to encode responses to *currently active frame deviations* that need to be discovered and interpreted. No matter how meaningful a conscious story may be, it always encodes perceptions and processing related to an immediate, often repressed, frame issue.

5. In general, people react paradoxically to therapists who are capable of securing their frameworks of psychotherapy. Therapists are well advised not to talk about a move to a private office with anyone but their patients, because doing so violates the spirit of the total confidentiality and privacy that are the essential aspects of the secured frame. As is true of some patients, colleagues and social acquaintances who learn of this kind of move are likely to try to undermine the frame-securing effort—the universal dread of secured frames activates many untoward responses. A common defence against the existential death anxieties stirred up in the

listener who is informed of a frame-securing move is to attack—
for other, overly rationalized, unconsciously driven reasons—the
therapist who is making the change.

Ms Roland, a depressed single woman in her mid-40s, was in
private therapy with Mr Adair, a social worker who saw patients in an office attached to his home. In the middle of a
session that took place in the second year of the therapy, Mr
Adair announced that he would be moving into a new office in
a month. He gave the patient the exact date of the move and
the address and telephone number of his new office. Ms
Roland, who was being seen once weekly on the couch, sat up,
took a pen and paper from her purse, and wrote down the
information as Mr Adair gave it to her.

Lying back again on the couch, the patient commented that
she thought she knew the office building that Mr Adair was
moving into—it was some sort of professional building, wasn't
it? When the therapist remained silent, she went on: she said
that she was thinking about her cousin, Lois, who had also
moved—from an apartment to a house in the suburbs. It was a
beautiful house with a lot of special features, like an indoor
grill for cooking and a huge master bedroom with two cedar
walk-in closets.

Lois was very happy there, but it didn't last. She developed an
acute infection of her pancreas and nearly died. Ms Roland's
thoughts shifted to her mother, who had died of a severe pneu-
monia when the patient was 3 years old. Her next thought was
of the death of her brother when he was 7 and the patient was
10. He died of meningitis after he had wandered into a warm-
up site where he didn't belong and had been accidentally hit
on the head with a baseball bat by a friend. It had happened
soon after their father had remarried and they had moved into
a nice house in which she and her brother for once had their
own bedrooms and they had a good family structure again.
Everything good seemed to come with something bad.

Mr Adair interpreted to his patient that she seemed to be reacting unconsciously to his announced move. Her images indi-

cated that she saw it as a change to a better setting, but she also seemed to be expecting that, while the move would be a good one and would stabilize their relationship in the therapy, some kind of disaster would follow—that she or he, or both of them, might even die. Ms Roland also seemed to be experiencing the move as an announcement of his loss or death and as a move into a forbidden place where she would be injured and die.

Ms Roland paused for a moment and said that she was now thinking about her grandmother who helped bring her up. She was a very wise woman who always had an answer to the problems that the patient brought to her. But she, too, had died suddenly, in a hotel fire when she was on vacation in Europe. Wisdom and death seem to go together, the patient mused. Perhaps that's her picture of the move—wise, but dangerous or potentially lethal. With that, the session was at an end.

In brief, in her first session in the new office, a private office space in which only Mr Adair practised, Ms Roland first said that she had nearly cancelled her session because she felt ill. The move seemed to be a bother—she had to drive an extra fifteen minutes to reach the new location. But now that she was here, she felt more comfortable in the new space, but it also seemed scary. At least there would be no more of those weird incidents, like the times she'd seen the therapist's wife and children before and after sessions. Once, her car had backed over Mr Adair's son's bike, and she was so embarrassed and upset she never told anyone about it.

Her themes in that session dealt with childhood fears of being alone, a man who stared at her through her bedroom window, and places where she had felt safe, protected, and cared for— but always with an addendum involving someone's illness or death.

This patient was especially vulnerable to secured frames and the existential death anxieties that they arouse. Her early traumas included the deaths of her mother and brother. These events had created an unconscious terror of annihilation in a secured space. She was nevertheless able to come to the new office and communi-

cate meaningful derivative themes that lent themselves to interpretation and deep insight.

Among the many universal meanings of Mr Adair's office
move, this patient selectively stressed the combination of security
and death-related trauma that she experienced in the newly
secured frame. She was under the influence of intense existential
death anxieties to a point where she felt physically ill, but she
was able to come to the first session in the new office space and
to continue the therapy. For her, the secured-frame issues were
far more conflict-laden and compelling than the frame-deviant
aspects of the move. The patient's unconscious perception of the
deviant side of the situation is nicely encoded in the allusion to her
brother's injury when he ventured into forbidden territory.

Some extremely traumatized patients have great difficulty tolerating a move of this kind. Their existential (and predatory) death
anxieties are so severe that their continuing the therapy is at issue.
They often break the frame unilaterally or ask the therapist to do
so. The therapist must use all of his or her sensitivities and frame-
managing skills to hold the frame steady and interpret the patient's
trigger-evoked anxieties. Properly done, these efforts enable these
patients to tolerate their activated existential death anxieties and
benefit from the experience of both surviving in the newly secured
frame and gaining new means of adapting to anxieties that have
plagued them virtually all of their lives.

Concluding comments

In some ways, living and working as a therapist in the world
defined by encoded derivatives and experienced by the deep unconscious system is far more arduous than living in the world
defined by manifest contents and experienced by the conscious
mind. The pursuit of deep unconscious experience and meaning is
a grim task that brings forth morbid images and powerful themes
that characterize the undefended and remarkably sensitive vision
of the deep unconscious mind, and touches on the severe secured-
frame anxieties and deviant-frame persecutions that unconsciously
terrorize both patients and therapists.

Were it not for the enormous cost of deviating, the highly defensive position and frame-modifying preferences of the conscious system might work well for a while. But sooner or later the violent and seductive aspects of frame breaking will destroy the illusion of gain achieved in this way. Unconsciously driven self-destructive actions by both patients and therapists are an inevitable consequence. It becomes clear that tolerating and understanding the world of deep unconscious experience and following the more disturbing and demanding dictates of the deep unconscious system prove to be the far wiser and, in the long run, easier course than living almost blindly in the world of conscious emotional experiences.

CHAPTER NINE

The setting
in public situations

There are, as we know, many kinds of public sector and organizational frames for psychotherapy, such as clinics, charitable associations, group practice arrangements, health maintenance organizations, and programmes offered by insurance companies, governments, churches, and hospitals. These settings, although often socially necessary, are characterized by a series of endemic compromises of the therapeutic frame that have disruptive consequences for all concerned. Managing these frameworks and offering a deeply constructive therapy experience under these conditions are challenging and often daunting tasks for the psychotherapist and counsellor.

Perspectives on clinics and similar settings

The social necessity for clinic-types of psychotherapy has blinded most therapists to their many drawbacks and prevented a careful search for the most optimal frames possible under these conditions. It is critical in exploring this sensitive subject not to allow social need to blind us to the natural and inescapable effects of modified frames. Human systems cannot escape psychobiological rules: the power of deep unconscious experience dominates emotional life regardless of conscious reasoning and need. The dilemma we experience in these situations stems from the essential design of the emotion-processing mind and pits the harm caused by all frame modifications against the need of many patients to be seen under compromised public and semi-public conditions. Therapists have an obligation to develop strategies that will resolve these conflicting pressures with as little harm and as much cure as possible for their patients—and as little grief as possible for themselves.

In this chapter, I use *the clinic setting* as my prototype of the essentially frame-deviant public and semi-public settings. While many of these modified settings are the only conditions under which a patient can receive therapy, they are frame-altered nonetheless—and the patient will experience them as such, vaguely consciously but intensely and clearly deep unconsciously. It is therefore important to avoid using these kinds of settings whenever possible and to minimize the deviant qualities of these situations when their use is inescapable. There is a tendency for therapists who practise under these conditions to engage in many unneeded frame breaks and to allow ancillary personnel to modify the frame in countless but avoidable ways. The more securely the other ground rules of therapy are maintained, the greater the healing powers of the therapist who works in a frame-deviant clinic setting.

Deviant features of clinic settings

In addition to the clinic setting itself, which is fraught with frame-related problems, many basic ground rules of therapy are also compromised in these settings. Patients experience clinic settings and ground rules with considerable deep unconscious perspective, especially when the deviations are kept to a minimum. The security provided to the patient by adhering to as many ground rules as possible implicitly encourages meaningful encoded communication by the patient and limits the detrimental effects of the core deviations. It is the arbitrariness of many clinic deviations that renders these settings particularly traumatic and troublesome for both patients and therapists alike.

The following are among the most common types of *frame breaks* that occur in clinics and similar situations (see also chapters ten to twelve):

1. The public waiting-rooms of clinics expose patients to countless strangers and sometimes to people they know. Conversations with other patients and therapists, and other clinic personnel, are common. They violate patients' needs for and rights to total privacy and confidentiality.

2. Secretarial areas and offices that are visible to outsiders allow patients to be exposed to third parties, to observe clinic personnel, and to overhear others speaking. These conversations may involve discussions of other patients, of clinic personnel including the patient's therapist, and of the patient himself or herself. The violations of privacy and confidentiality are striking, deeply affecting, and at times blatantly offensive and hurtful.

3. Clinic offices are usually poorly soundproofed, if at all. Many offices have glass in their doors or windows which allows others to see into the interior of the office. These arrangements modify the privacy of the therapy.

4. Therapists may be required to use different offices for sessions with the same patient. They may also be asked to work in rooms that serve as entrances to other offices so that other patients and therapists walk through the therapy room to get to their own therapy spaces.

5. Records related to the patient's sessions, which modify their privacy and confidentiality, may, in addition, be placed where they are in full view of other patients, or they may be openly carried about by therapists, filed by secretaries, or available for perusal by others.

6. The presence of third parties is inherent to clinic psychotherapies. The possible intruders include outsiders as well as other

therapists who treat or see the patient along with the primary therapist. Multiple therapists are not uncommon in clinics, with patients being seen individually and in groups, or in treatment with both a talking therapist and a medicating doctor. Patients may be assessed and processed in group meetings and may be presented at rounds or conferences, often with the patient present. The violations of privacy, confidentiality, and the one-to-one therapeutic relationship are massive and chaotic.

Access by third parties to clinic records is typical. In some instances, this includes a patient's employer or fellow employees. In addition, third-party contaminations in the form of supervisors and educators are frequent features of clinic settings. The patient's material may also be used for other kinds of teaching, and for research as well as publication; these partially justifiable deviations are, nonetheless, frame-breaking.

In clinics (and in some private therapies), in addition to a designated patient, often other family members are in therapy with the same or another clinic therapist. Also, friends or other relatives may be attending the clinic, as may other doctors whom the patient either sees or has seen professionally or knows socially. Third-party contaminations are boundless.

7. Compromises of the therapist's relative anonymity through overheard conversations or via information directly conveyed to the patient by a third party to the therapy are also common in clinics. In addition, because deviant settings tend to beget further deviant framing activities, modifying frames becomes *the basic mode of emotional adaptation* for both patient and therapist. Thus, a therapist may share personal information with a clinic patient even though he or she might not do so with a private case; or, a patient may suddenly be unfaithful to his or her spouse, in part unconsciously because the deviant mode of coping is being unwittingly supported by a frame-deviant psychotherapist.

8. Clinic fee arrangements almost always involve departures from the ideal frame. The patient's fee may be paid by a third party, or there may be no fee at all, or the fee may be low or reduced specifically for the patient after frame-deviant negotiations.

Patients typically pay their fees to third parties such as secretaries or financial officers.

Responsibility for all sessions being the patient's is seldom the rule, and therapists are more inclined to cancel sessions than they are with private patients. Other aspects of the relatively fixed frame, such as the time, frequency, and duration of sessions, are also likely to be compromised.

The list of frame modifications common to clinic settings seems interminable. Working with *manifest* reactions to these deviations is quite ineffective. Lacking a safe setting and set of ground rules, patients seldom refer directly to a frame modification, even when it is blatant. Nevertheless, *encoded* narratives conveying the patient's deep unconscious sensitivity to and processing of the deviant-frame impingements do appear from time to time. Monitoring the status of the frame and offering trigger-decoded interpretations when the patient's material permits—and rectifying unnecessary frame deviations when possible—presents these patients with the best possible therapeutic experience that they can hope for under these trying conditions.

Some common problems

Doing sound psychotherapy in a clinic setting is far more difficult than it is in private practice. The many frame modifications experienced by these patients tend to make the therapy an unsafe place for self-revelation—manifestly as well as on the encoded level. The setting thereby interferes with the essential verbal-affective conscious and deep unconscious working over of the background and activated frame issues on which a sound, insightful, and holding–containing cure is based.

Communicative resistances are ever-present—evident triggers go unmentioned, and encoded communication is constricted. Patients' use of *maladaptive psychological defences*, such as extremes of denial and repression, are also quite typical. Subjected to excessive frame breaking, clinic patients invoke frame modifications themselves whenever they are anxious or in conflict. The predominance of frame-modifying adaptations makes for a chaotic psychotherapy and external life for the patient. Absences, latenesses, leaving sessions early, complaining about the therapist to others at the clinic, and similar kinds of frame breaks by patients are frequent. Often, the patient turns to these deviations soon after the therapist has deviated and has failed to understand and interpret the responsive encoded material.

As noted, under clinic conditions, patients seldom refer directly to an acute frame break, even when it is quite blatant and as recent as minutes before a particular session was to begin. The therapist must therefore be alert for *encoded allusions* to disturbances in the conditions of the therapy. Playback of these encoded derivatives organized around a known active frame-deviant trigger is a frequent intervention. This work often proceeds on the deep unconscious level, with repeated playbacks of derivative themes without the activating trigger ever being manifestly articulated.

In this connection, there is a major and almost unresolvable problem with therapeutic work in these modified settings. Unconsciously, patients hold their therapists responsible for all of the communications from, and actions by, other clinic personnel. But quite often *the therapist is entirely unaware of what has transpired between the patient and other employees*. The third-party contact is itself frame deviant, but quite often the intruding individual has done something additionally deviant to compound the situation— for example, told the patient something personal about the therapist, excused the patient from timely payment of the fee, or suggested that they go out for a coffee. These are frame-deviant events that impact strongly on the patient, yet they are unknown to the therapist.

These kinds of triggering events are seldom referred to directly by the patient. As a rule, the patient will convey heavily disguised, derivative allusions to the incident, but the unknowing therapist will be hard pressed to organize and decode the themes properly. A blind playback of the encoded themes organized around the therapist's best guess as to the nature of the trigger may be offered to the patient. Clinical experience, however, shows that this type of intervention seldom prompts the patient to refer directly to the missing trigger or effectively to work through unconsciously the effects of the deviation. Detecting and rectifying these frame-deviant secrets is an ever-present challenge for the clinic psychotherapist and counsellor. Training clinic personnel to avoid frame-deviant behaviours seems the best antidote to this problem—an effort that often meets with notable resistance because clinic workers tend unconsciously to be strongly invested in frame-deviant modes of coping.

A final note: none of this implies that psychotherapy cannot be successfully carried out in clinic settings. Properly conducted according to the principles articulated in this book, and with allowances for secured-frame moments, much healing can transpire. Patients deeply unconsciously experience and process the ramifications of these deviant frames, but they also have an unconscious perspective on their necessity and they experience deep unconscious perceptions of a therapist's constructive efforts made under these difficult conditions.

Mrs Ray was in psychotherapy at a clinic with Ms Earl, a social worker. In a session early in the therapy, the patient spoke about her personal financial problems and a recent rent increase she had been asked to pay which seemed illegal to her. This led her to think of a situation at work in which an auditor came to check the books of her company and accused the bookkeeper of stealing money missing from the petty cash. The accusation proved to be false. It turned out that the owner of the company had borrowed the money because he was short of cash and had forgotten to put it back.

Mrs Ray made no manifest allusion to a frame-related trigger as she continued to associate. Ms Earl recognized the main frame-related themes in her patient's narratives—money, intruder (the auditor), stealing, and false accusation. In attempting to find a triggering event for these encoded themes, Ms Earl was unaware of any recent third-party intrusion into the therapy. Contact between the patient and the clinic secretary did, however, take place each time the patient came to the clinic because the patient was obligated to pay the fee to the secretary before each session began. But Ms Earl was not aware of a problem with the patient's fee, or of a false accusation that had been made to the patient by herself or anyone else.

When the patient mentioned that she was getting weary of being in therapy, Ms Earl used this general bridge to therapy as an opportunity to play back the frame-related themes in the patient's material. Mrs Ray responded with confusion and failed to discover a trigger for the imagery. On that note, the session ended.

By coincidence, after the session Ms Earl happened to go past the clinic secretary's work area. The secretary caught her attention and said that she owed Ms Earl an apology. It seemed that before her session that day, when Mrs Ray had come to her to pay her fee, the secretary had brought up an unpaid balance. The patient protested that she was not in arrears, and, after a tense discussion, the secretary said that she would look into the matter but was fairly certain that her records were right. While the patient was seeing Ms Earl, the secretary discovered a book-keeping error—the patient was right and she was wrong. The secretary said she'd straighten things out the following week.

Paying receptionists in advance for sessions is a frame modification frequently adopted in clinics. In a secured frame, patients pay their therapists directly, doing so after the sessions have been held—usually paying for their previous month's sessions at the beginning of each new month. The policy of making payment to third parties and in advance of sessions is frame-deviant (see chapter eleven). This practice of pre-payment is justified by clinic personnel by citing the vast amounts of money that clinics would fail to collect if they used the ideal ground rules for payment—once-monthly, for the sessions of the previous month. Nonetheless, this custom is frame deviant and has evident destructive implications—the basic mistrust of the patient high among them. Patients' deep unconscious experiences of this deviation are reflected in images of exploitation, greediness, and mistrust.

In the vignette, unknown to Ms Earl, the patient was encoding an emotionally charged triggering event that had transpired just minutes before the session had begun. The trigger involved the secretary, who, in the patient's deep unconscious mind, is identified with—is the same person as—the therapist. On this level, then, it is the therapist who has modified the frame and falsely accused her patient.

Under these circumstances, patients usually shift to intellectualizing without generating encoded imagery, or they present narratives that contain heavily disguised themes that are all but impossible to decipher. In this situation, however, the therapist was able to surmise from the patient's relatively clear derivatives that some issue had arisen with the patient's fee. Yet even though the therapist made a reasonable playback of the relevant themes to the patient, the triggering incident remained repressed and unreported. The patient's deeply unconscious mistrust of the therapist, which was based on the deviant setting and other frame modifications of her therapy, undoubtedly contributed to her communicative resistances.

Notice, too, that the deep unconscious meanings of these transactions would go entirely unrecognized by a therapist who listens and formulates in terms of manifest contents and their implications and does not engage in trigger decoding. Clinics have proliferated and operated with overly deviant frames and excessively modified ground rules because their therapists are not trained to appreciate the realm of deep unconscious experience—and all of its many effects.

Some clinical precepts

Because clinic therapies are fundamentally frame deviant, most of the therapeutic work with deep unconscious experience revolves around the deviant-frame conditions of the therapy and active frame-modifying interventions made by the therapist or other clinic personnel. Virtually all of a patient's meaningful psychodynamic issues and their genetic connections are activated in the immediate situation with the therapist. They arise and present themselves for interpretation and resolution as part of a patient's conscious and unconscious adaptive responses primarily to framing occurrences—deviant and secured—and secondarily to the nature of the other efforts of the therapist. The inner mental world and past history of a patient cannot be truly comprehended without an understanding of the immediate trigger, within therapy, that has activated a particular constellation of external perception, inner experience, and genetic recall. Because these triggering events are organizing and giving form to the patient's intrapsychic responses, they are the keys to understanding what the patient is trying to communicate and adapt to—both now and in the past.

As examples, a secretary may tell a patient something personal about his or her therapist; a patient may see his or her own or someone else's chart; or words may be heard coming from a therapist's office while the therapist is seeing another patient. These acute frame breaks are traumatic and damaging to the patient, who deeply unconsciously feels betrayed and violated. Although seldom mentioned directly, the patient will always process these hurts in his or her deep unconscious system and communicate encoded themes that reflect the damage being done.

This harm, however, can be counterbalanced by sound interpretive work by the therapist and rectification of the frame break if possible—and by holding secured other aspects of the frame. Without these interventions, however, the patient is left with a deep unconscious experience that provides an unconscious impetus towards neurosis and maladaptation. On the other hand, sound therapeutic work in the presence of basic frame modifications creates a competition between two sets of unconscious perceptions and introjects of the therapist—one set harmful, the other set healing. When frame deviations are kept to a minimum, the positive qualities of the therapist's work will win out.

In light of the predominance of frame deviations in clinic therapies, a critical principle of technique calls for *affording each clinic patient the experience of frame-securing moments at one or more junctures in his or her therapy*. Existential forms of death anxiety are universal sources of conflict and emotional maladaptation. No psychotherapy can be thought of as relatively complete without providing a patient with an opportunity to deal with frame-securing triggers and the conflicts, anxieties, and memories that they activate—they are quite different from those aroused by deviant-frame triggers.

These much-needed, secured-frame moments materialize when a therapist can secure an unneeded deviation—for example, by changing from having a secretary collect the fee from the patient to arranging for the therapist do so. Or the secured-frame moment may come about when a therapist uses the patient's encoded directives as a basis for holding the frame secured when the patient asks for an unnecessary frame modification—for example, an unjustified change in the fee or in the time of a single session.

Typically, the patient will respond to this type of frame-securing intervention with encoded validation via positive images of wise and truly helpful people. As we have seen, these images are usually followed by themes of entrapment and annihilation. This constellation reflects the encoded affirmation of the enhancing effects of the securely held frame and the existential death anxieties that these frames evoke. The imagery will also include dynamically and genetically meaningful material that touches on the patient's death-related life experiences and the anxieties and conflicts that they have caused. These issues can then be interpreted and worked through in light of the immediate frame-securing triggering event. In all, this is a highly salutary therapeutic experience for patient and therapist. Both parties deeply unconsciously experience the therapist as someone who can successfully cope adaptively with existential death anxiety—a most curative realization.

The ideal session

There are two basic forms of *communicative resistances* (Langs, 1997) and both occur frequently in patients seen in clinics. These resistances can best be understood and appreciated by developing a model of the ideal, communicatively non-resistant session. This model is constrained by the evolved architecture of the emotion-processing mind. That is, by design it is impossible for a patient directly to state his or her deep unconscious experiences, and they can be conveyed only through encoded themes. Thus, communicatively, the ideal session has two essential features:

1. The patient at some point alludes *manifestly* to a frame-related intervention by the therapist—frame-securing or frame-modifying.

2. Through narrative images, the patient expresses in encoded form his or her unconscious experience of the intervention. The themes should include both *bridging imagery* that links the themes in the manifest story to the nature of the latent, frame-related trigger, and *power themes*—the damage package (e.g. themes of death, illness, harm) and sexual themes—that convey its meanings.

Such material meaningfully embodies a patient's selectively experienced, valid deep unconscious perceptions and processing of the universal implications of a therapist's frame-related intervention. With material of this kind available for interpretation, the therapist needs only to link the trigger to the themes to enable the patient to understand his or her deep unconscious experience. When available as encoded directives in the patient's imagery, rectification of a frame deviation would complete the therapist's efforts.

Departures from this ideal communicative network reflect *communicative resistances*.

Typical communicative resistances

In clinic psychotherapy, ideal communicative networks are seldom available to the therapist. This form of resistance is in small measure a result of intrapsychic conflict. In the main, however, it arises as an adaptive response to the deviant conditions of clinic psychotherapy in which violations of privacy and confidentiality render unconscious communication unsafe and unwarranted. Unconsciously, these patients are in conflict between, on the one hand, their basic need to encode responses to therapists' errant frame-modifying interventions for healing purposes and, on the other, the need to protect themselves from the harm caused by these encoded revelations through the lack of privacy and the like and from the frame-deviant therapist whom they cannot trust to tolerate, without revenge, the patient's encoded perceptions of the therapist in light of the implications of the prevailing frame modifications.

The usual solution to this conflict is that a patient will resist communicatively for extensive periods of time, but will occasionally encode a response to a trigger at a time when the trigger also is alluded to directly—a moment at which the communicative resistances are put aside.

The following are the most common means through which a patient's communicative resistances materialize in a given session:

1. The active frame deviation is not mentioned manifestly. When this occur, two possibilities exist:

    a. The encoded themes are readily decodable, and they organize strongly around the immediate frame deviation. This enables the therapist to play back the derivative themes in the hope that this effort will enable the patient to allude manifestly to the trigger—after which a full interpretation and, at times, frame rectification are possible.

    b. The encoded themes are dense, difficult to decode, and weak. In these cases, the therapist should remain silent and wait for clearer material. On occasion, the therapist may offer a weak playback of the encoded themes in the hope that the patient will then reduce his or her communicative resistances and allude to the trigger and/or convey stronger and clearer derivative themes. This intervention is seldom successful, however, because a clinic patient's resistances are usually strong and unconsciously motivated.

2. The second form of communicative resistance is seen when a patient alludes manifestly to a frame-deviant triggering event, but the encoded images are weak and difficult to decode. In this type of situation, the trigger is clear but the encoded images are unworkable. Often, the themes lack power and deep meaning, and their bridging qualities are weak. Under these circumstances, the therapist has no recourse but to remain silent—if necessary, for the entire session. In time, the patient will create a session in which both a frame-modifying trigger and strong encoded themes are available for interpretation and frame rectification.

Unrectifiable frame modifications

In clinic psychotherapies, many of the aspects of the frame, including the setting, cannot be rectified by the therapist. This fact has important ramifications.

First, when patients consciously and unconsciously realize that little or nothing will be done about a frame modification, they are reluctant to allude directly to the frame break or to encode their perceptions of the harm that these deviations are causing. They also invoke communicative resistances in connection with these uncorrectable frame deviations because unconsciously most patients try to spare their therapists undue psychic pain and guilt (see below).

Second, in situations where the therapist intervenes properly and decodes a patient's derivatives in light of a frame-deviant trigger, there is an activation of a severe conflict because of the therapist's inability to rectify the situation even though the patient's encoded themes point to this need. As a result, the patient will encode a small measure of validation in response to a sound intervention, but then react with negative imagery and fresh resistances because of the therapist's failure to follow through with what the patient has asked for and truly needs—that is, a frame-securing moment.

Third, patients do have a perspective on these situations, in that unconsciously they feel both helped and hurt when a therapist understands a frame-deviant situation but is unable to offer an uncompromised setting and cure. The mixed image of the therapist as both sensitive and insensitive is, nevertheless, "crazy making" and disturbing to the patient. Moments of this kind, with their essential contradictions, frequently prompt patients to terminate their clinic therapies prematurely.

Therapists who do not trigger decode are seldom faced with this kind of problem. They are insensitive to the importance of a given frame break, fail to appreciate the patient's encoded responses, and do not understand the patient's need for frame securing. The therapy proceeds without a recognized deep unconscious dimension, and all the while the therapist is seen deeply unconsciously by the patient as insensitive and hurtful—deeply insightful understanding and holding are seldom experienced.

Reducing clinic deviations

Therapists can undertake many measures that reduce frame deviations in clinic psychotherapies to an absolute minimum. I
concentrate here on setting-related deviations and reserve for further chapters the means by which other aspects of the frame can be
kept maximally secured under clinic conditions.

The following are some of the ways in which clinic settings can
be made as secured as possible:

- Soundproofing offices and closing-off offices from view from
  hallways or other outside areas.

- Arranging for small waiting areas near each individual office so
  that patients are less exposed to each other and to outsiders and
  other therapists.

- Creating private secretarial areas so that records are not exposed and conversations are not overheard.

- Arranging that telephones can be turned off when patients are
  being seen in session.

- Placing conference-rooms away from where patients wait for
  and see their therapists.

- Locating clinics in professional buildings or in buildings of their
  own.

This sample of corrective measures expresses a spirit of respect
for the framework of psychotherapy and, thereby, for the patient's
deepest therapeutic needs. It is all too seldom realized that concerns for the frame are identical with concerns for the patient. It is
the failure to appreciate the ramifications of the ground rules that
most neglects the needs of patients—in clinics and private therapy
alike.

Additional problems for clinic therapists

Finally, I offer a brief look at some of the special problems faced by
therapists who work in clinics. The first of these comes from the
finding that deviant settings unconsciously encourage and support

deviant needs and modes of adaptation in both patients and therapists. This means that clinic therapists are more likely than therapists in private practice to make deviant choices when faced with a frame issue and that, similarly, patients are unconsciously encouraged to utilize frame-modifying modes of adaptation as well.

Because patients in clinics suffer from frame deviations, especially those that are gratuitous, and therapists suffer with unconscious guilt when they harm their patients, clinic therapists should be especially alert to their own frame-modifying tendencies. Patients are particularly disturbed when a therapist's personal inclinations to modify rather than secure a ground rule compounds the basic deviant qualities of a clinic psychotherapy. Thus, whenever a clinic therapist is offered a choice between two or more framing responses, he or she should carefully weigh the possibilities and try to select the least deviant frame-related interventions (see chapter fourteen).

The second problem for clinic therapists is also technical, even though it is driven by deep unconscious needs. Because their patients' material is often strongly critical of them personally, clinic therapists are unconsciously motivated to defend against recognizing the active frame-deviant triggers that are creating these damaging images. Similarly, these therapists are also inclined to miss the unconsciously conveyed, encoded meanings of the disparaging disguised images that their patients convey in their narrative material.

Alertness to frame-related triggers and to encoded meanings becomes a vital necessity for clinic therapists. They are also well advised to engage in self-processing (Langs, 1993) in order to deal deeply and effectively with the inevitable conscious and especially unconscious conflicts and guilt that the harmful aspects of working in clinics always creates for therapists. These are the main counter-measures available to clinic therapists as means of overcoming their counter-resistances.

Another relatively unresolvable problem inherent to clinic settings involves the personal deep unconscious experience of the therapist. Because the use of these settings always does some degree of damage to the patient (and to the therapist himself or herself), guilt, and especially *unconscious guilt*, are continual problems for clinic therapists. This guilt motivates therapists to behave in self-punitive ways with both patients and figures in their out-side lives. As a result, therapists are inclined to make unneeded frame breaks and erroneous interventions as unconscious ways of inviting patients to do harm to themselves. In response to the unconsciously perceived unconscious wishes of their therapists, clinic patients may abruptly terminate or disappear from their therapies or complain to administrators about their therapists. Requests to change therapists are also not uncommon under these conditions. These behaviours often cause therapists a great deal of pain and embarrassment. Indeed, similar unconscious invitations to others to cause them harm occur in the clinic therapist's personal life, usually without insight into their deep unconscious, guilt-ridden sources.

Such are the trials and tribulations of clinic psychotherapists and counsellors. Although fraught with pitfalls and disturbing unconscious transactions, clinic practice is one of the most challenging and potentially rewarding experiences that a psychotherapist can have—the more difficult the unconscious issues, the greater the possible gain in fresh insight and self-understanding.

CHAPTER TEN

The time dimension

Regardless of the locale of a given psychotherapy, the ideal ground rules call for a definition of various time factors. Managing this seemingly simple aspect of the frame is, however, beset with potential problems. As with any ground rule, the overall goal is to secure this aspect of the frame to the greatest extent feasible, to minimize frame alterations, and to interpret and, if possible, where needed, to rectify those modifications that do exist.

The time, length, and frequency of sessions

The temporal dimensions of the ground rules of psychotherapy are an essential part of the relatively stable, fixed frame. The main components are:

1. *The duration of sessions.* Sessions should last 45 or 50 minutes in standard forms of psychotherapy. This convention, which

may have arisen for monetary reasons, has psychological support in that it allows sufficient time for meaningful communications, however limited (Langs, 1993).

Once the length of sessions is established, it should be adhered to with utmost strictness—the deep unconscious system is sensitive to the slightest variation beyond a few seconds or so.

The following are some basic technical principles connected with this aspect of the frame (see chapter eleven for a more complete discussion of the initial contact and first session):

a. During the first telephone call, the therapist should offer a time for the consultation that can be used by the patient in an ongoing basis if he or she decides to enter therapy. The therapist should inquire as to the patient's general availability for sessions and should propose a single possibility and then offer another if the patient is unable to make use of that time slot. The length of the consultation session should also be indicated by the therapist, so that the patient is aware of this aspect of the frame and is introduced to secure-frame interventions.

b. A therapist should not see a patient in consultation unless he or she has a suitable time available for ongoing therapy. The ill-advised practice of seeing a patient in consultation in order to select another therapist for the patient is a vested-interest deviation that deeply unconsciously—and sometimes consciously—is experienced by patients as hurtful, greedy, rejecting, seductive, and assaultive. There is no sound basis for this frame-breaking practice.

c. All of a patient's sessions, including the consultation session, should be of the same length.

d. Care should be taken to begin and end sessions as scheduled. Stopping a session prematurely is seen unconsciously, if not consciously, as dismissive and punitive. It is also unconsciously understood to be a result of the therapist's fear of being trapped with the patient and as reflecting a dread of the unconscious perceptions of the therapist that the patient has been working over in the session at hand. If the error is not caught and the length of the session actually shortened, ideally the fee for the session should be reduced proportion-ately. Providing the patient with the lost time by adding it to the following session is a commonly used corrective, but it modifies the aforementioned set length of sessions and speaks unconsciously for the greed of the therapist. If in-voked, the patient's deep unconscious perceptions of the deviant aspects of the corrective should be recognized in his or her derivatives and properly interpreted in light of the deviant trigger.

Extending a session for any reason is seen unconsciously by patients as seductive and entrapping, and as a loss of contact with reality on the part of the therapist. Consciously, patients often feel flattered with the implied interest shown by their therapists, but deeply unconsciously their reaction is very negative.

A therapist should have no qualms about interrupting a patient who is in the midst of a thought or story when time is up. This is generally done by simply announcing "Time is up" at the appropriate moment. The therapist then rises, stands in place, and allows the patient to leave on his or her own; in principle, it is the therapist who should close the door(s) to the consultation-room after the patient has left that space. Therapists should remember that every frame-securing event—even ending a session on time—stands among the most healing efforts that a therapist can offer to patients.

2. *The day and time at which sessions are held.*   The day and time of the sessions should also be firmly set for the duration of a therapy. A personal emergency or other need experienced by a patient or therapist does not call for a change in the hour or for a make-up session. Only two exceptions to this rule can be supported, both of which involve a modification of the frame in order to re-secure it:

a. If a patient has a major change in life circumstances—for example, a change of job or, for a student, in the schedule of classes—the therapist is obligated to change the time and possibly the day of the sessions lest the patient be forced into a premature termination of the therapy. A full exploration of this anticipated trigger should occur well in advance of making this frame change. Despite the realistic needs of the patient, which lead to conscious appreciation of the shift, the deep unconscious experience will centre around the deviant aspects of the frame modification—its seductive and manipulative qualities. When these themes appear, they must be linked to the trigger and properly interpreted to the patient.

Once a change of this kind is made, it should be sustained as part of the newly established, secured frame. If, later on, the patient becomes free at the previous time of the sessions, the therapist should *not* return to the old time. Such a move is experienced unconsciously as frame deviant and severely exploitative and seductive.

If the therapist cannot accommodate the patient's new schedule—and every effort should be made to do so—termination may prove to be inevitable. If so, the patient should be entirely responsible for his or her next decision, whether it is to forego therapy entirely, seek a new therapist, or wait for the present therapist to find a suitable hour for resuming the therapy—and the responsibility for checking for this possibility belongs to the patient and not the therapist. At no time should a therapist change the hour of another patient to accommodate a patient with this kind of scheduling problem.

    b. If a therapist's life or work situation changes, he or she may be forced to change the day and/or time of a patient's sessions. Every effort should be made to avoid such changes, but when they are unavoidable they should be permanent rather than temporary. This type of vested-interest deviation is experienced unconsciously as self-serving, manipulative, and seductive, and as an abandonment that disregards the therapeutic needs of the patient.

    3. *The frequency of sessions.* This dimension of the temporal frame is also set firmly in the consultation session and sustained throughout the therapy.

    a. The most common pressure to modify this aspect of the ground rules arises at times of emotional crisis when a patient appears to be decompensating, or becomes homicidal or

THE TIME DIMENSION 155

suicidal. The request for an added hour or a shift to more frequent sessions per week may come from the patient or therapist.

In these situations, it is well to recognize that holding the frame secured is, in general, far more therapeutic than any type of frame modification. Furthermore, in most instances, a background frame deviation and/or an immediate frame break are playing an important role in the creation of the emergency. This means that further frame modifications are likely to aggravate rather than improve the situation. Ultimately, the best solution lies with interpreting and rectifying the underlying frame modifications and holding the frame secured.

When a life may be at stake, however, deciding on the side of safety and arranging for an extra session or an increase in the frequency of sessions—or even more extreme measures like hospitalization—may be the wisest course. The patient will react to added sessions as a loss of holding and containing, a failure of the therapist to sustain a secured frame in the face of pressures to deviate, an inability of the therapist to manage the therapy under existing conditions, and as an exploitation and seduction. Hospitalization is usually experienced unconsciously as an assaultive rejection and therapeutic failure—there is always a strong measure of trauma involved. Nevertheless, if the deviation is necessary, there will also be deep unconscious appreciation reflected in the patient's encoded narratives. It is, in principle, far better to err on the side of modifying the frame rather than risk the life of the patient or someone else.

b. Requests to reduce the frequency of sessions involves a frame modification that is seldom justified. If a twice- or three-times-weekly patient asks to be seen less often each week because of a financial setback, the change may well have to be made. Even so, it will be experienced deeply unconsciously as a frame break and will evoke unambiguously negative images and meanings. While, in theory, patients who are overly sensitive to secured frames may also request a reduction in the frequency of sessions, this is seldom the case—the holding qualities of the sound framework usually make secured-frame anxieties tolerable.

The request to reduce the frequency of sessions as a prelude to termination is a maladaptive frame break that generally serves as a defence against the existential death anxieties aroused by the anticipation of the end of treatment and the losses that it entails. It is a proposed frame alteration that is best explored and interpreted in terms of the patient's encoded themes, which will always point to holding the frame as set.

c. Therapists who work with the communicative approach find once-weekly psychotherapy a powerful and effective therapeutic modality. Therapists who have faith in their healing abilities within this type of framework are able to deal with problems related to the time and fee for sessions more easily than those inclined towards more frequent weekly hours. The practice of reducing one's fee if a patient comes to therapy more often than once weekly is ill-advised. It is a highly seductive, exploitative, self-sacrificing frame modification, and, despite the conscious flattery that some patients experience, the deep unconscious effects are quite negative.

d. If a therapist falls ill or has an emergency and expects to miss a single session, he or she should simply miss the hour without notifying the patient (Langs, 1997). This secured-frame approach is difficult for many therapists to accept because they mistakenly use manifest contents and social standards—rather than therapy-related criteria—for their framing decisions. Nevertheless, reaching a patient by telephone modifies the proper locale of contact between patient and therapist and is experienced deeply unconsciously by the patient as an assaultive and seductive intrusion. While consciously disturbing, adhering to the ground rules of therapy under trying conditions in which existential death anxieties are activated is enormously appreciated and healing on the deep unconscious level.

In situations in which there is a sudden need for an extended or indefinite absence and the therapist cannot get to the office to see his or her patients, it will be necessary to modify the frame by contacting them by telephone. Under these conditions, every effort should be made to see to it that the therapist is the person who makes these calls. If this is not possible, the calls are best made by another professional rather than a family member (Langs, 1997).

4. *Responsibility for sessions.*   The patient is expected to attend and be responsible for the fee for all scheduled sessions. For his or her part, a therapist is entitled to take a judicious number of vacation days—not doing so is both frame deviant and unbearable for both parties to therapy. As a rule, the amount of time a therapist is away from the office should not exceed four to six weeks in the summer and two to three weeks in the winter. All vacation plans should be announced two or more months in advance so that patients can make their own plans accordingly. The vacations of the therapist are, in unusual fashion, interruptions in the flow of sessions and in that sense frame-altering, but essentially they are part of the secured frame. These separation experiences are strongly evocative of existential death anxiety and will need to be interpreted as such.

Mr York, a young man with obsessive symptoms, was seeing Dr Ryan, a male therapist, in psychotherapy at a clinic. A year into the therapy, Dr Ryan needed to cancel a session with Mr York because of an acute illness. He elected to call the patient at work and reached him there, telling him that he was ill and needed to cancel the hour.

In the following session, the patient mentioned the cancellation and said that he hoped that Dr Ryan was feeling better, and Dr Ryan nodded yes. For the remainder of the hour, Mr York ruminated about what kind of illness the therapist might have had. He spoke at length about how illness can interrupt work and pleasure, doing so without recounting specific stories. In the absence of clear or powerful encoded themes, Dr Ryan remained silent.

In the next hour, Mr York did not allude to the cancellation, but he did comment that the therapist looked well that day. After a pause, he said that he was thinking of a bizarre thing that had happened to him yesterday. A strange looking, huge man had broken into Mr York's office. The man thought he was in someone else's office, though it wasn't clear who that was. He kept muttering, "Do something, can't you see how sick I am?" Mr York didn't know what to do. The man was spacey and looked very ill, as though he had a brain tumour or Alzheimer's disease.

The patient was frightened of the man, but also furious. Somehow, Mr York managed to get him to leave. He screamed at the man to get the hell out of his office! It was a weird scene: Mr York's telephone kept ringing, but he didn't dare pick it up to see who was calling. He was afraid the man would murder him if he did. As suddenly as he had appeared, the man turned and left the office—he never should have been there in the first place.

When further material did not add appreciably to the pool of themes and the patient did not refer directly to his call to the patient, Dr Ryan intervened with a playback of encoded themes. His comment went like this:

"You mentioned that I looked well today [beginning with the general bridge to therapy and with a manifest theme that bridges to the latent, frame-deviant trigger of the telephone call to the patient] and went on to allude to someone who intruded into your office. You also mentioned that your telephone kept ringing [the best encoded representations of the frame-deviant telephone call and a reference to one of its strongest meanings—intrusion]. You also referred to illness and the fear of being harmed. Something connected to me and therapy has evoked these images."

Mr York laughed and said that Dr Ryan must be talking about that telephone call he had made to him to cancel the session two weeks ago. He was surprised that he was still reacting to it. He then said that the images seem to fit—maybe he was a little annoyed by the whole thing.

Dr Ryan pointed out that his images actually indicated that he was more than annoyed, that he was furious and that he had felt assaulted by the call and saw the therapist as a deranged man, intruding into his space. The patient responded by saying that for some reason he was thinking of an experience he had had in college. He was taking a course with an excellent biology teacher who was real smart in a lot of ways and almost always on the mark. But on one occasion the teacher did a strange thing: in the course of a meeting that Mr York had with him in his office about his class work, the teacher revealed that he was suffering from cancer of the throat. The confession was very off-putting—it seemed like a misplaced cry for help.

Dr Ryan interpreted that the patient's picture of a "real smart" professor indicated that he—Dr Ryan—had been on the mark with his prior comments. But the patient was now adding that his revelation on the telephone that he was ill had been experienced unconsciously as an inappropriate, off-putting, assaultive, sick self-revelation. Mr York was letting him know that he saw it as a cry for help from his patient, who objected strongly to it. In fact, everything about the call seemed to have been experienced as assaultive and crazy and out of place. Mr York's images were indicating that Dr Ryan should refrain from making such calls in the future, and the therapist indicated that he would go along with his patient's recommendation.

This vignette illustrates the deviant-frame qualities of a therapist's telephone call to a patient and of a self-disclosure of illness as well. We see, too, an example of the kind of communicative defences that are found so often in clinic patients: in the first session, the patient manifestly represented the frame-deviant trigger, but failed to generate strong derivative themes; then, in the second hour, he developed strong encoded themes but failed to produce a direct reference to the trigger. In this case, the playback of derivative themes enabled the patient to lift the repressive barrier and mention the trigger manifestly. Specific interpretive work and rectification followed—the patient was afforded a significant secured-frame moment.

At times of a temporary illness, then, allowing the absence to be experienced when the patient arrives at the therapist's office and finds that the therapist is not there appears to be the most frame-securing approach to this difficult moment. This unconsciously validated precept stands against the consciously experienced insensitivity that this action will evoke in some patients. In light of the nature of the personal trauma, a therapist's preference for deviating when faced with this death-related problem is somewhat understandable. But doing so will most certainly be deeply unconsciously perceived and processed by the patient as a frame break, and the responsive encoded themes and negative deep unconscious experience will need interpretation. In addition, using the patient's encoded directives, the therapist must also rectify the deviation by expressing his commitment not to call again if a similar emergency were to arise in the future.

5. *The duration of the therapy.*   While defining a specific length of a therapy is not a part of the established frame, the expected length of therapy is nevertheless a temporal dimension of treatment. It has several notable features:

a. The ideal therapy is *implicitly* arranged to continue until the patient has insightfully and constructively resolved his or her emotional maladaptations and wishes to terminate the therapy. The treatment is therefore open-ended, and eventually the *patient* sets the time for termination and determines just how long the termination period will be. Often this decision will be first expressed in encoded, derivative form and will need suitable interpretation by the therapist in the context of the anticipated trigger constituted by the therapist's acceptance of the patient's decision to end the therapy.

b. Short-term therapies entail departures from this unconsciously sought ideal, even when the duration of therapy is agreed upon by patient and therapist from the beginning of treatment. As a result, on the *deep unconscious level*, the central adaptive issue for the patient (and therapist) in these therapies is the pre-fixed duration of the treatment. Most, if not all, of the patient's conflicts and resistances will emanate from and be organized around that core frame issue—and around other deviant aspects of the treatment as well. The deep unconscious experience of this deviation is usually reflected in themes of abandonment and harm, selfishness and disregarding the needs of others, exploitation, omnipotent control, and the like. Much needed secured-frame moments are very rare in this type of therapy experience.

c. Therapists in private practice with their own office space should have full command over their schedules. As a result, problems with respect to the duration of a given psychotherapy should be relatively infrequent. They arise largely when the patient or therapist is involved in a major catastrophe or a move away from the locale in which the treatment is being conducted.

The overall situation is rather different for most clinic and many managed-care psychotherapies. Often, clinic policy will set the duration of treatment, and it is likely to entail a premature termination of the therapy. These frame-deviant, forced terminations evoke a wide range of conflicts and are extremely hurtful for all concerned: they are difficult to work through on the deep unconscious level. Existential and predatory death anxieties are very strong when a therapist abandons a patient for any reason. However, in private practice, leaving a patient is usually permanent, whereas, in clinic psychotherapies, in many instances a forced termination leaves open the possibility of continuing with the therapist in his or her private office. This is often the best choice among frame-deviant possibilities (see chapter fourteen). Similarly, many therapists who see patients under managed-care conditions that limit the number of sessions in the therapy often elect to continue the treatment privately. In most instances, this is a far less traumatic frame deviation than the alternative of ending the therapy before the patient has achieved a reasonable cure.

Ms Turner, a woman in her 30s, was in private psychotherapy with Dr West, a woman therapist, because of a long-standing drinking problem and depression. She worked in an art gallery and was being seen at 2 p.m. on Mondays, the day that the gallery was closed.

In her second year of treatment, Ms Turner lost her job but soon found employment at another gallery, but this was, however, open on Mondays. In the session after she accepted the offer of this new job, the patient asked the therapist if she could be seen on Tuesdays since that was her new day off. As she planned to start her new job in two weeks, she needed to have an answer rather soon.

Dr West responded by asking Ms Turner to continue to say whatever came to mind. The patient's thoughts went to an incident that had happened some two weeks earlier. She had rented a summer house by the ocean and went to the local town hall to obtain a beach permit. To her surprise, on the first day that she used the permit she got a parking ticket. Enraged, she went back to the clerk who had told her that she could use the permit for all of the town's beaches. The clerk admitted that he had made an error, and went on to say that even though it wasn't legal for him to do so, he would fix the ticket if the patient wanted him to. It was one of the few times that Ms Turner had allowed herself to be involved in breaking the law; it would have been crazy to do anything else.

Dr West interpreted the themes in this story as the patient's unconscious commentary on the expectation that she would agree to the proposed frame modification. She would be violating a law—a ground rule of therapy—but, given the circumstances, it would be justifiable and the sensible thing to do.

Ms Turner nodded her head and then commented that, despite his mistake, the clerk at the permit office was really very bright. Ms Turner had enjoyed talking to him. Before she left, the clerk implored Ms Turner not to tell anyone about what he was going to do. If word got out, there'd be endless demands to fix tickets—it would be a mess.

Dr West took this addendum as encoded validation of her intervention because it contained an allusion to a well-functioning individual and provided an insightful warning that frame modifications beget frame modifications—and that it would not be wise to modify the frame further.

This vignette captures the mixed qualities of a *forced frame modification*—it is necessary and fair, but it does break the rules. Such are the mixtures that reality often brings into a psychotherapy experience.

CHAPTER ELEVEN

The first session
and fees

T he ground rules related to the fees for psychotherapy are, in
principle, stated in the first session. But before the fee is
dealt with, there is an initial contact with the therapist,
usually via a telephone call for an appointment to arrange the
consultation session. Many aspects of these initial contacts are
overlooked consciously by both therapists and their patients, even
though they are processed intensely by the deep unconscious
systems of their respective minds. For this reason, I offer a brief
discussion of the initial contact before turning to the ever problematic area of managing the fees for psychotherapy.

The initial contact

The therapist's handling of the first telephone call and the consultation session sets the tone for the entire psychotherapy. The rules
that prevail for the call and the first hour are identical to those that
apply to an on-going therapy. The only notable difference between

the initial session and all other sessions is that the therapist will spell out the basic conditions and ground rules of the therapy largely without the encoded directives of the patient. In all other sessions, with the rare exception of a frame break discovered privately by the therapist, his or her frame-management efforts should be based on the patient's encoded models and recommendations, which are always directed towards securing the frame. But because both patient and therapist must have a clear framework for the therapy from the outset, the ground rules need to be stated at some point in the first session, even in the absence of suitable encoded material from the patient.

With respect to the ideal, secured frame pertaining to the first telephone call and initial hour, the main points (see also, Langs, 1982, 1992) are as follows:

1. The appointment for the first session should be made in response to a telephone call *from the patient*. In all settings, the arrangements should be made by the treating therapist with the person who is to be seen in therapy. Departures from this practice involve third-party contaminations that are acceptable only in a dire emergency—for example, arranging a first hour with a third party in order to see someone who is suicidal and refuses to call the therapist for an appointment.

    • As is true of any departure from the ideal frame, deviations that occur during the initial telephone call to the therapist will need both interpretation and rectification in the first session, or as soon as the material from the patient permits. For example, if a third party has made the initial appointment, the patient's encoded narratives—and they will be abundant in the first hour—should be used to secure the frame by interpreting how the derivatives indicate that there should and will be no further contact whatsoever with third parties to the therapy.

2. If possible, the consultation session should be held at a time that the patient will find acceptable if he or she decides to enter therapy. A change in time at any point in therapy is a frame modification, although it is quite workable if the new time involves the second and all subsequent sessions.

3. The therapist should greet the patient in the waiting-room, introduce himself or herself, and allow the patient to find his or her way into the consultation-room, closing the door(s) behind them. In clinic settings, it is imperative, if at all possible, to find the patient without the therapist announcing the patient's name aloud—this is a hurtful exposure of the patent to third parties and an inappropriate way to initiate a therapy. Because a handshake involves physical contact, however non-sexual and socially acceptable, it seems best to confine the initial greeting to a verbal acknowledgement.

4. In all cases, even when the therapist anticipates recommending that the patient lie on a couch, the first session should be conducted in face-to-face fashion. The therapist's office should be arranged so that the chair on which the patient should sit is self-evident. If the patient moves towards the therapist's chair, it will be necessary for the therapist to indicate where the patient should sit.

    a. Once the patient and therapist are settled into their respective chairs, the therapist should initiate the session with a query such as: "With what can I be of help?" The patient is then allowed to speak and say whatever comes to mind, and the therapist should listen attentively. If the patient blocks early in the hour, the ground rules regarding free association and lack of censorship should be explained. As the session proceeds, however, it is often possible to interpret the patient's resistances in terms of a prior frame-related trigger, be it deviant or frame-securing; this frame issue may pertain to the first telephone call or to the basic conditions of the therapy. In any case, deep unconsciously, the patient is well aware of the ideal frame, and the encoded themes will point the way for the therapist's interpretation and rectification, if need be.

    b. It should be understood that as the patient *manifestly* tells the story of why he or she is in need of treatment, *latently* the patient is encoding responses to the frame impingements—secured or deviant—that have developed prior to and during the consultation session. The therapist should therefore be aware of all identifiable frame issues that have already arisen in the therapy and be prepared to interpret and rectify them as needed, using as much of the patient's derivative material as possible.

5.   About half-way into the first session, the therapist should state his or her recommendation that therapy is indicated for the patient and offer to provide it. Once the patient accepts the therapist's proposal, the therapist should proceed to establish the ground rules of the therapy. This is usually begun by stating the fee, which should be in keeping with the therapist's level of expertise and the fee structure of the community of therapists in the area in which he or she works. A single fee should be stated, and the fee should not be negotiated, reduced, or increased.

a.   Closely connected to the fee is the frequency of sessions. Communicative studies indicate that once- or twice-weekly sessions are ideal. Once weekly treatment, which is standard for empowered psychotherapy (Langs, 1993), is a highly viable mode of healing in that considerable deep uncon-scious processing of unconscious issues transpires between sessions, and their essence can be captured and worked through in the weekly hours. Twice weekly therapy may be indicated when there are acute emotional problems and the patient is able to afford the therapist's full fee for both ses-sions. The practice of a therapist reducing the patient's fee to enable the patient to be seen more than once-a-week is frame deviant and deep unconsciously perceived by the patient as seductive, exploitative, and self-sacrificing on the part of the therapist.

b.   In dire situations in which a patient clearly cannot afford the therapist's stated fee, the therapist does best frame-wise by suggesting a referral to someone who will accept a lower fee. The alternative recommendation is the offer by the consult-ing therapist to see the patient at a reduced fee, but this frame modification may be difficult to work through. As a frame-deviant intervention fraught with negative unconscious meanings for the patient, it can seriously compromise the basic conditions of therapy and interfere with the curative process. Nevertheless, many therapists *with trigger-decoding skills* try to work with these patients once weekly by reducing their fee, and they find that their efforts sometimes meet with success.

The reaction of patients to this type of frame change varies. Some patients will work through the deviation, especially if the therapist has secured the frame in all other respects; there may then be a positive outcome to the therapy. However, other patients will exploit this basic frame modification by unilaterally altering other aspects of the therapy frame or acting out with frame deviations in their everyday lives. They also may attempt to extract more frame deviations from their therapists. When, in keeping with the patient's encoded derivatives, these frame changes are not granted by the therapist, some of these patients will leave treatment. Those who do so almost always suffer from severe secured frame, death anxieties and have a history of over-intense death-related traumas. They are difficult to treat under any conditions, and they stay in therapy only if the frame is compromised— in which case, the therapist is inadvertently supporting the patient's pathological, frame-modifying basic mode of adaptation.

6. To continue the outline of the first session: once the patient has agreed to the asked-for fee, the therapist should indicate that the fee is to be paid at the beginning of each new month for the previous month's sessions. The therapist should then state the remaining ground rules of the therapy, as follows:

  • The patient should be informed of his and her responsibility for the time allotted for the sessions and for the fee for each scheduled session. The day(s) and time(s) of the sessions should be established, and the therapist should indicate that the time has been set aside for the patient and that it will be reserved for the patient for as long as he or she wishes to continue the therapy. It should also be made clear that these are fixed times and that both parties to the therapy are committed to being at the sessions when scheduled. If the therapist has specific vacation plans, they should then be announced to the patient. If not, the patient should be informed of the therapist's usual vacation policy.

Where necessary and appropriate, the ground rules related to privacy and confidentiality should be articulated, whereas the therapist's relative anonymity and the absence of physical contact are usually explicated implicitly (see chapters twelve and thirteen). In essence, through both statement and act, the therapist indicates his or her devotion to the patient's cure via deep interpretations and secure framing efforts in ways that find encoded validation and enhance the security of the therapeutic space.

Dynamically oriented therapists should recommend the patient's use of the couch. This part of the secured frame speaks for the pursuit of deep unconscious meaning.

Finally, the fundamental rule of free association and the need to avoid any kind of censorship are stated to the patient. In this connection, departures by the patient from these two tenets should be dealt with by the therapist through interpretations made in light of activated triggers because they are, as is true of all resistances, *interactional events*—so-called *resistance patient-indicators*, with contributions from both parties to therapy.

The main resistances to these precepts, should they appear, usually involve the use of the couch and issues related to who will be responsible for the payment of the fee—and, in clinics, who will collect it. Patients who are fearful of deep unconscious meaning tend to be reluctant to lie on the couch. The therapist should merely recommend its use, and the patient has the right to accept or not. If the patient elects to sit up, this act is another *resistance patient-indicator*, an indication of a therapeutic need within the patient—in short, a need to have an intervention from the therapist. As such, the patient-indicator is likely to lend itself to both interpretation and rectification. With judicious and sound therapeutic work, the patient is likely to take to the couch after a while and benefit from the insights developed in the course of the exploration of his or her reluctance to do so.

The fee

With this as our foundation, we can now turn to the specific issues related to the fee that a patient pays for psychotherapy or counselling. Managing the fee of a psychotherapy is a difficult responsibility for the private psychotherapist and a source of endless problems for clinic therapists and their patients. In the private therapy situation, the very fact that a therapist is dependent on the patient for part of his or her income is a burdensome reality for both parties to treatment. In addition, money is a commodity that causes no end of grief for those who are involved in its pursuit—it is one of the prime sources of interpersonal and social conflicts, and of disturbances in an individual's inner state and self-esteem. The need for a suitable income often motivates therapists to break frames in ways that are harmful to their patients—and to themselves.

The following are some of the fundamental clinical precepts that apply to the fee:

1. The therapist should have a basic, usual fee that, in principle, he or she charges all patients. In situations of evident hardship, the therapist may privately decide to ask for a fee that is slightly lower than his or her accustomed fee. At the appropriate moment in the first session, the therapist should state a particular fee as his or her fee, with no indication that a concession is being made when such is the case. The timing of the patient's payments—at the beginning of a month for the previous month's sessions—is then indicated (see above).

2. Although this aspect is seldom mentioned directly, the expectation is that the patient alone will be responsible for the payment of the fee, which should be made by cheque to the therapist directly. It is left to the patient to bring up the question of third-party payers or other fee issues.

3. If the patient indicates that he or she wishes to use insurance or other means of third-party payment, the therapist should, in principle, respond by indicating that the patient should continue to say whatever comes to mind. If necessary, the therapist can explain to the patient that all decisions regarding the ground rules of therapy should be made in light of the material that comes from the patient as it illuminates the patient's conscious and unconscious views of the proposal.

    a. Typically, patient are split with respect to third-party payers.

Consciously, most patients simply want third-party coverage, rationalizing that it is needed to enable them to be in therapy and that it is their due. They fail to appreciate consciously the deep unconscious motives behind their wish, nor do they understand the impact that these arrangements will have on them and their therapy on the deep unconscious level. Third-party payers unconsciously prompt the creation in patients of virtually unmodifiable defences and resistances—intruders into the highly charged therapeutic space make the revelation of both conscious and unconscious secrets and truths extremely risky and often quite untenable.

In contrast to conscious preferences for this deviation, every patient deeply unconsciously has a clear comprehension of the need for a secured therapy frame and of the harm caused by this violation of the ideal ground rules. Patients' encoded themes always speak for securing the frame and not including a third-party payer. The violations of privacy and confidentiality that accompany outside-payer arrangements will manifestly and deep unconsciously disturb the therapy experience in critical ways.

b. The absence of full responsibility for the fee and the accompanying leakage of information to outside parties, which violates the total privacy and confidentiality of a therapy, have devastating effects on the patient and treatment experience. The patient's communications become shallow, flat, lacking in power themes and deep unconscious meaning, and are confined to superficialities and trivialities. From time to time, the patient will encode one or two devastating images related to the deep unconscious meanings of this frame violation, and interpretation and eventual rectification are necessary responses from the therapist. Failure to do so will make deeply insightful cure virtually impossible.

Therapies in which third parties are fully or in part involved in the payment of the fee are very common today largely because psychotherapists are frame-insensitive and suffer from unrecognized secured-frame, death anxieties. They avoid deep unconscious meaning and are willing to settle for highly defensive and self-hurtful attitudes and the use of non-validated interventions.

c. There is a set of typical themes and unconscious perceptions that follow a patient's request for a third-party payer. They involve images of inappropriate exposure, such as a doctor examining the patient in front of family members; betrayals of trust; greed and exploitation; lack of privacy; and harmful intruders. There are, as well, clear encoded models of rectification. Interpretation and rectification undertaken on the basis of these themes always obtain encoded validation, but they also arouse the patient's secured-frame anxieties and activate past traumas whose unconscious meanings and connections to the present will require interpretation.

d. Once the work of interpretation has been carried out and the encoded frame-securing directives acknowledged, patients fall into two groups: those who consciously appreciate the situation in depth and forego the insurance, and those who see the point but deny its importance and continue to insist on the outside payer's involvement in the therapy. These latter patients tend to be secured-frame-sensitive and to have histories of significant death-related traumas that have yet to be mastered. Unconsciously, they are terrified of the experience of entrapment and the existential death anxieties that will be mobilized were this deviant aspect of the frame secured.

The material from these patients will repeatedly encode the negative and damaging consequences of the presence of the third-party payer, even as he or she continues to use conscious-system denial to sustain the frame-deviant therapy situation. If the therapist continues to interpret the patient's material in light of the proposed deviation, the patient, terrified of a secured frame, may leave treatment. But, on the other hand, if the therapist agrees to accept the insurance, the patient is consciously delighted, but deeply unconsciously disillusioned. The therapist is unconsciously seen as violating his or her own principles and commitments, and as being fearful of the secured frame himself or herself. The therapist is experienced as being useless and hurtful to the patient, and termination is likely. The therapist—and patient—are very much on the horns of a difficult dilemma.

Slow and patient interpretation, along with restraint with respect to invoking the necessary frame-securing elimination of the third-party payer, is the therapist's best strategy. This may allow the patient sufficient time to work through his or her severe death anxieties and dread of the secured frame to the point where the elimination of the third-party payer can be tolerated. In these cases, the positive therapeutic effects of this work are considerable because the issues that the patient resolves touch closely on those that have been derailing his or her emotional adaptations and relationships with others in everyday life.

e. In clinic settings, charging low fees and making arrangements through which secretaries and other clinic personnel collect the fee have damaging effects similar to those seen with third-party payers in private practice. These deviations motivate clinic patients to refrain from communicating narratives with deep unconscious power and meaning, and from revealing their deep unconscious views of their therapists and the repressed secrets that account for their own emotional dysfunctions and lives.

f. Driven by unrealized deep unconscious needs, patients use third-party payers as a way of undermining truly insightful forms of therapy. For their part, therapists—gravely concerned with earning a living and fearful of secured frames themselves—are all too ready to accept insurance payments without exploring and fathoming the deeply unconsciously mediated negative effects that this frame break has on their patients and themselves.

Patients' deep unconscious needs for punishment are also unwittingly exploited by these frame breaks, and untold harm is done to patients and those with whom they have relationships in their daily lives. The frame modification persists largely because these detrimental effects are split off from their deep unconscious sources and subjected to defensive denial by both patients and therapists—but the harm is real, nonetheless.

4. The patient should be held responsible for the fee for all scheduled sessions. This responsibility is essential to the secured

frame and is deeply linked to existential death anxiety in that it is an important source of the patient's necessary and therapeutic sense of entrapment. This feature of therapy offers the patient an opportunity to deal with his or her existential death anxieties—a major source of emotional dysfunctions in every human being.

* * *

Mr Flynn, an unmarried man in his 40s with obsessive-compulsive difficulties, was in once-weekly, private psychotherapy with Mr Howe, a social worker. In the eighth month of treatment, the patient lost his job as a computer programmer. He had some savings and immediately began to look for new employment. It was in this context that he came to a session and began by asking Mr Howe to reduce his fee until he had found a new job and stabilized his life. The therapist responded by suggesting that the patient continue to say whatever came to mind.

Mr Flynn's thoughts went to another time when he had lost his job. He had borrowed money from his brother to get through the crisis. But the situation turned sour because lending the money made his brother nasty and impossible to be with. His brother became very demanding and asked for a lot of favours; he even wanted Mr Flynn to work in his business for a menial salary—so small that it would be like slave labor. The patient regretted borrowing the money; it was a great mistake, and it ruined his relationship with his brother.

Mr Howe interpreted that the themes reflected how his patient would experience a fee reduction. He would see it as a destructive loan of money and as his—the therapist's—working for a menial sum that would engage him in slave labor. Contrary to his conscious request, Mr Flynn's unconscious commentary and recommendation was that it would be a great mistake to lower the fee because it would ruin their relationship and the therapy.

Mr Flynn nodded his head in agreement and recalled a

situation in which he had been asked to lend money to a friend who was out of work. He somehow felt he'd never get the money back and decided it would be best for his friend if he did not do it. The friend quickly found a good job. Some time ago, Mr Flynn had tried to borrow money from his father, who had turned him down. Upset at first, Mr Flynn suddenly came up with a new idea at work which earned him a bonus. Indulgence seem to discourage motivation to be creative and grow. As for now, he'd see how long it took him to find new work. He had some savings, so he could continue the therapy for a while and see what happens.

Still out of work, some weeks later Mr. Flynn felt a renewed sense of financial pressure. He found out that his insurance coverage through his former employer was good for six months after he left the company, and that 80% of the cost of his psychotherapy was covered by the policy. Based on material that had emerged in an earlier exploration of using the insurance for the fee for his therapy, he had elected not to use it. But now things had changed, and he wanted Mr Howe to fill out an insurance form so he could get reimbursement for the last three month's sessions.

When it was offered to him, Mr Howe did not accept the form, but again suggested that the patient continue to say what came to mind. An incident from his childhood, from about age 12, popped into Mr Flynn's thoughts. He had gone to the beach with his parents and brother. When they went to change into their bathing suits, his father noticed a pimple on the patient's penis. His brother heard his father making a fuss and looked at the patient's penis, laughed aloud, and made jokes about the patient having syphilis. But the worst part of it was that after he put on his bathing suit and left the locker room, his father took the patient aside and called his mother to look at the pimple. Although the patient resisted, the father managed to expose him to her. It was incredibly humiliating. Mr Flynn lost all trust in his father and didn't talk to him for weeks; and it was months before he could look his mother in the eye again.

Mr Howe made the interpretation that the story encoded how Mr Flynn would unconsciously experience his accepting the insurance company into the therapy. Mr Howe would be exposing Mr Flynn inappropriately to third parties, much as his father had done with his mother. It would be experienced as a way of humiliating him in front of others and cause the patient to lose trust and not want to communicate to the therapist any longer.

The patient responded with a story of a college room-mate who had once kept Mr Flynn covered when their fraternity brothers tried to undress him at a co-ed party. Mr Flynn then acknowledged that his images and themes seem to support the idea of not introducing the insurance company into his therapy, but he insisted that he would have to terminate the therapy without the coverage.

Three weeks later, despite a large number of additional encoded stories that spoke against the measure, including several images that indirectly via encoded themes advised termination until the patient could again fully pay for his therapy, Mr Howe gave in to his patient's pressures and filled out an insurance form. Stories of greed, betrayal, exposure, seduction, and murder soon emerged.

In the sessions that followed, the patient made additional demands for frame modifications, and when Mr Howe held the frame secure based on Mr Flynn's encoded directives, the patient became angry and non-communicative. Within a month, despite efforts at interpretation and an attempt to re-secure the frame with respect to payment of the fee (carried out at the behest of Mr Flynn's encoded themes), Mr Flynn left therapy. The week before he left, he messed up a job interview. In his final session, Mr Flynn said he'd return once he found a job—but whether he does remains to be seen.

Frame modifications beget frame modifications; frame breaking soon becomes the preferred mode of adaptation. The therapist who understands encoded meaning and the need for secured frames, who trigger decodes and manages the ground rules at the behest of the patient's encoded directives, creates a self-contra-dictory situation of maddening chaos when he or she acts in opposition to a patient's deep unconscious directives and decides to compromise the frame for any reason. Reality is the context for life, and real hardships do exist, but frames are also part of—and a crucial context for—reality. Frame breaks, no matter what the basis, cause damage and interfere with the pursuit of cure based on sound holding–containment and deep insight.

The best a therapist can do when frame modifications are inescapable is to keep them to a minimum, interpret their meanings as the patient's material permits, keep the remainder of the frame secured, and re-secure the frame as soon as possible. In working this way, the helpful side of the equation may well outweigh the hurtful side.

Therapists who do not understand trigger-evoked unconscious communication and the nature and functions of the ground rules may shift about, one minute unwittingly and arbitrarily holding the frame, the next minute violating it. The chaos this creates is tolerated through denial—the patient has no conscious apprecia-tion for the deep unconscious aspects of the situation, and the therapist is derivative-deaf. The therapy hours are filled with trivi-alities, as well as with unempowered manifest contents and their all too evident implications. Some patients may gain a measure of relief in this way, doing so via the frame modifications and non-validated interpretations that reinforce their use of defensive denial and offer them pathological forms of gratification. But the relief comes at a great though often unnoticed price—psychoso-matic symptoms, self-hurtful actions, and unexplained symptoms, in particular.

As therapists, we may wish nature were otherwise—but what is, is. Managing the relatively fixed frame is part of the real and substantial context and holding environment of a patient's psycho-therapy. When a therapist establishes a safe, secured, and creative space, the patient will flourish, though he or she will also inevita-bly be compelled to deal with deeply disturbing but powerful secured-frame-related, deep unconscious perceptions, conflicts, and existential death anxieties—though under conditions that fa-vour their insightful resolution.

When, in contrast, a therapist establishes an unsafe, insecure therapeutic environment, the holding is of poor quality, the introjects of the therapist are damaging to the patient, and relief is essentially maladaptive, fragile, and insubstantial. A therapist's framing decisions and activities with respect to the relatively fixed frame and especially the fee are a major determinant of a patient's therapeutic experience and its deep success—or failure.

CHAPTER TWELVE

Total privacy
and total confidentiality

We turn now to the more fluid and less precisely definable aspects of the framework of psychotherapy. In this area, the ground rules of total privacy and total confidentiality undoubtedly are two of the most crucial and yet most often violated conditions of therapy, even though they are ardently sought, on the deep unconscious level of experience, by patients and therapists alike. Therapists who trigger decode patients' material cannot help but be impressed by the enormous power that these two aspects of the ground rules exert on the therapeutic process and the lives of their patients—and on themselves. In this chapter, I present the position of the deep unconscious system on these two ground rules and attempt to explain why these invaluable safeguards are so often ignored and violated.

Total privacy

While, in general, total privacy and total confidentiality go hand in hand, they tend to stress somewhat different aspects of the ground rules of psychotherapy. Total privacy calls for a treatment situation that involves only the patient and therapist, and excludes all manner of outsiders. Ideally, it implies a referral from a professional or other neutral source; a private waiting-room and office; a separate exit from the consultation-room, or spacing sessions sufficiently apart so as to preclude contact between patients; the exclusion of family members connected with the patient or therapist; payment for all sessions by the patient alone, using his or her own, personal funds and chequing account; a one-to-one relationship and interaction, without others present or reports to others; and, on both sides, the absence of note-taking, recordings, supervision, or presentations or discussions with any other individual.

Total privacy has features that are intertwined with total confidentiality. For example, the ground rules call for sessions that go unrecorded except in the minds and memories of both parties to therapy. Also required is that neither the patient nor the therapist speak to any outsider about any aspect of the therapy sessions. These tenets ask for a mixture of total privacy and total confidentiality that inherently serves to safeguard against the communication of the transactions of sessions to any third party. This canon is violated not only through the physical presence of another person in the treatment setting, but also through conversations or written contact with others about any aspect of the therapy. Even reporting back to a referral source—whether verbally or in writing, by the patient or the therapist—violates this ground rule.

Total confidentiality

While it seems self-evident that total confidentiality is a *sine qua non* for the effective pursuit of cure through deep insight and sound holding–containing, psychotherapists appear to have devalued its importance and created unfounded rationalizations to excuse and justify their seemingly endless modifications of this vital ground rule of psychotherapy. Total confidentiality provides a closed and protected setting and container for the patient's conscious and unconscious revelations. This ground rule, as it interlocks with the rule of total privacy, assures the safe communication of the patient's conscious and deep unconscious, manifest and encoded, messages and secrets—expressions of guilt, anxiety, conflict, perception, memory, and the like. It also protects the therapist from the self-hurtful disclosure to others of his or her errors and failings—and even his or her effective therapeutic work—a protection that must not, of course, be the basis for careless interventions or harmful techniques.

Trigger decoding patients' material in light of adaptation-evoking interventions by therapists reveal that, on the level of deep unconscious experience, patients are highly perceptive and remarkably creative and effective in utilizing their adaptive resources. The deep unconscious system perceives and processes the most terrible and awesome selected meanings, truths, and other implications of the actual behaviours and communications from therapists—including those that sustain or violate the confidentiality of a therapy.

We are reminded that deep unconscious experience and processing deals with unconscionable traumas and harm from others; one's own most grevious assaults, blunders, and seductions; the predatory intentions of others and oneself; experiences of unbearable guilt for harms real and imagined; and much of the awful awareness of the inevitability of death for oneself and others. These are issues and conflicts that evoke inner feelings and images that are terrible to behold within the therapeutic setting, especially when they pertain to the therapist and his or her deviant-frame interventions. It is destructive to evoke such images by violating patients' need for, and right to, total confidentiality and unthinkable to allow these perceptions, fantasies, and memories, however directly or indirectly expressed, to leak out of the therapist's office in any manner whatsoever—yet it is an everyday occurrence.

There are, of course, gradations of the violation of total confidentiality. So, it must first be understood that, basically, a frame is either secured or modified, and that any degree of compromise in confidentiality is a frame break that will have deep unconscious

effects, in keeping with all such deviant-frame measures. In addition, these effects will be consonant with the therapist's particular
violation of the patient's confidences, and the more severe the
break, the more intense the consequences for both patient and
therapist.

For patients, therapists' violations of total confidentiality will
be experienced unconsciously as betrayals, inappropriate expo-
sures, breaches of trust, self-serving and exploitative acts, abuses
of and assaults on the patient, sexual abuse, and the like. For the
therapist, no matter how much the frame break seems justified, the
deep unconscious experience is one of having done these terrible
things to the patient. Deep unconscious guilt is strong, and it will
lead to self-punitive acts and interventions and, at times, ill-advised undue efforts to repair the damage done to the patient
through additional frame breaks. These misguided actions pathologically gratify the patient and therapist, but on the whole they
cause further harm and create terrible vicious cycles of damage
begetting damage. True reparation comes only from trigger-decoded interpretations and frame rectifications.

Factors in patients' reactions to frame breaks

As is true in connection with all of the ground rules of psychotherapy, violations of the total privacy and confidentiality of a
therapy will have effects related to the following factors:

1. *The fact that a ground rule has been modified.* This refers to the
    universal consequences of all frame breaks and therefore to the
    experience of all patients and therapists. There is in all cases the
    loss of safety, holding, containment, trust, and the like, as well
    as the instinctualization of the patient–therapist relationship.
    The experience is one of betrayal, harm, and seduction by the
    therapist.

2. *The consequences of the violation of the specific ground rule that has
    been modified.* Each type of frame break has its own universal
    meanings and implications. For example, violations involving

the time of a session have a set of particular consequences that are different from violations of total privacy, and both differ in some of their effects from modifications in the relative anonymity of the therapist.

3. *The current status of the therapy within which the frame break occurs.* This includes the current overall state of the framework of the therapy; the nature of recent frame-related and non-frame interventional triggers; and conflicts and issues that exist between the patient and therapist.

4. *The history of the therapy, especially the vicissitudes of its framework.* Patients react differently to frame modifications depending on their prior frame-related experiences with their therapists. A history of many frame deviations leads to one set of unconscious perceptions and consequences, whereas the context of an otherwise stable and secured frame leads to quite another set.

5. *The attitude of the therapist towards the frame break and his or her frame-related preferences.* A therapist who is prepared to deal with a frame deviation and to interpret the patient's encoded material—no matter how devastating to the therapist—and who is ready to secure the frame to the greatest extent possible will evoke one type of deep unconscious reaction from the patient. These responses are very different from those obtained by a therapist who is insensitive to the patient's encoded material and deep unconscious reactions to frame issues, and who is inclined towards a frame-deviant mode of adaptation and towards doing therapy under frame-modified conditions.

6. *The status of the patient's inner mental world, the nature of his or her life history, including early frame-related experiences, and his or her preferred frame-related mode of adaptation.* Patients' own life histories and framing experiences and preferences play a significant role in how they react to their therapists' frame modifications. Also critical is a patient's history of death-related traumas and how they were handled by all concerned.

Notable, too, are the strengths and weaknesses of the patient's adaptive resources and the type of intrapsychic and interpersonal conflicts that the therapist's recent interventions have activated in the patient. These historical and inner mental and interpersonal factors play a role in the extent to which a patient responds to a frame deviation with encoded material; in the degree of disguise of these derivatives, the selection of those meanings of the deviation to which he or she is most sensitive; in his or her tolerance for, or refutation of, the frame break; in the patient's resultant attitudes and behaviours related to the therapy; and in the emotional consequences of the frame modification.

At one extreme, there are patients who will find conscious reasons to terminate a therapy in which a therapist has created an unanalysed and/or unrectified frame deviation—never realizing the deep unconscious, frame-related sources of the unconsciously justifiable decision for premature termination. At the other extreme are patients who will endure without conscious protest, though with ample deep unconscious objections, any number of blatant and harmful frame breaks by a therapist. These patients are likely to be unconsciously terrified of secured frames and deeply troubled by unconscious guilt and needs for suffering and punishment.

Common violations

A list of frequent modifications of the ground rules of total privacy and confidentiality will afford us a sense of the issues involved regarding these tenets. I list these classes of frame violations together because they almost always go hand in hand. They include:

1. Perhaps the most common departure from the ideal one-to-one relationship and total privacy of private therapy involves *third-party payers*—parents and other relatives of patients of all ages, insurance companies, health maintenance organizations, governmental agencies, medical plans, and so forth. In most cases, total confidentiality is also modified through the release of information about the patient and the therapy. This may occur in small amounts (e.g. giving the dates of the sessions) or

through extensive reports (e.g. providing the status of the so-called transference, the patient's main problems and diagnosis, a psychodynamic formulation, a treatment plan, prognosis, etc.).

The intrusion of a third party into a psychotherapy reduces the patient's commitment to the therapy. More tellingly, however, it compromises the therapeutic hold and renders the therapeutic space unsafe, especially when it comes to revealing conscious and unconscious secrets, perceptions of the therapist, traumatic early-life events, encoded derivatives, and virtually everything else that is critical to an insightful, frame-holding cure.

As noted earlier, the uncontrolled proliferation of therapies lacking in total privacy and confidentiality stems not only from enormous reality pressures, but also from a vast array of deep unconscious, maladaptive needs and failings in psychotherapists. These include monetary greed, loss of clinical acumen when income is threatened, personal unresolved frame-deviant preferences and secured-frame death anxieties, failures to appreciate the critical importance of deep unconscious experience and the functions and effects of the ground rules of therapy, and an inadequate sense of the power of the deep unconscious factors in emotional adaptations and their malfunctions. These maladaptive needs and oversights are so prevalent, so strongly reinforced by a therapist's peers and his or her own therapy and therapist, and so in keeping with the pathological needs of patients and present-day society at large, that they seem impenetrable to much-needed change.

On the surface, insurance companies feel more than justified in seeking reports about the therapies that they sponsor and in arranging for peer and other types of reviews. Therapists have failed to argue convincingly for patients' inviolable needs for total privacy and confidentiality, and they have not established themselves as trustworthy. Their primary concern has been with their own financial needs rather than the therapeutic needs of their patients. They have also been confused on the issues involved, and unfortunately some therapists are dishonest in completing insurance forms. Neither therapists nor insurance companies have any palpable idea of the enormous harm that is being caused by the frame modifications that they conspire to make standard for the field.

In time, disaster will befall the field of psychotherapy and its patients and therapists. But it is likely to take decades or more before the significant sources of failed therapies are located in their frame modifications and therapists own up to their responsibilities in this regard. The situation is grim: the field of psychotherapy needs an effective frame-securing crusader.

2. A related modification of privacy and confidentiality involves parents, relatives, or friends of patients who attempt to speak to or meet with their therapists. This type of frame break occurs quite often in therapies in which the therapist accepts third-party payments. It is also standard practice for therapists who have been trained to see the parents and other relatives of youthful patients in sessions that are held with or without the patient present—a type of intrusion that is quite rare in secured-frame therapies.

Technically, a therapist should not hold a conversation or meet with a third party under any circumstances. The therapist who receives a call from a third party and happens to answer the telephone should simply indicate that it is not appropriate for him or her to talk to the caller. If a therapist receives a message on an answering machine from a third party, the call should *not* be returned. The patient should be informed of the call relatively early in the following session, but not until the patient has begun the session and revealed what is on his or her mind.

The only possible exception to these rules of non-contact with outsiders pertains to callers who report the danger of suicide or homicide in a patient. This very event tends to happen mainly in therapies with substantially deviant frames. Still, it must be kept in mind that a frame violation *is* a frame violation—even when a life is at stake. Such contacts should, then, be kept to a minimum and fully explored and interpreted with the patient—and the frame break rectified as soon as possible.

3. Another extensive source of third-party intrusions into therapy involve supervisors and mental health professionals who are party to presentations of a patient's sessions by his or her therapist. This type of deviation may involve individual or group supervision, presentations at professional and public

meetings and seminars, and writings that appear in books, journals, magazines, and elsewhere. The deviation is not eradicated through the use of disguise, and it is aggravated by asking permission of the patient to present such material.

There are, to my knowledge, only three justifications for this type of modification of the total privacy and confidentiality. The first is a therapist's need for personal therapy, in which he must free-associate and may thereby allude to his or her patients. The second is the educational need of every psychotherapist to learn to do psychotherapy by presenting supervisors with the transactions of therapy sessions—though the case material should *not* be recorded in any manner, because this creates unnecessary added deviations to the already deviant supervisory situation (Langs, 1994). The third involves the pressing need for a formal science of psychotherapy and psychoanalysis, which can be achieved only through quantitative research, for which the clinical session must be recorded so that all of the data is available for study. But here, too, it must be appreciated that the therapist so engaged is involved in a significant frame deviation that patients will react to with extensive deep unconscious perceptions and processing activities. These are much-needed but risky therapeutic situations in which the needs of the therapist and the field of psychotherapy are given precedence over the therapeutic needs of the patient— a decision whose deep unconscious consequences must not be ignored.

With regard to supervision, the interests of both the patient and the therapist are served by supervisory presentations, in that the educated therapist functions better with his or her patients than one who is untrained. It is important, however, not to compound this deviation by informing the patient of its occurrence or asking for his or her permission. Patients are, however, unconsciously and sometimes consciously aware of the intrusion of a supervisor. On rare occasions, they directly refer to the supervision, but in most instances their awareness of the presence of a supervisor is unconscious and is encoded in the themes of their narratives. Alertness to themes of third parties, observers, students, teachers, intruders, and such is essential under these circumstances—a most difficult task for any therapist who is being supervised. In any case, as the patient's material permits, the student–therapist should offer playbacks of the relevant encoded themes organized around the unmentioned, third-party supervisory trigger.

Recording sessions for research purposes is a special deviation that has many unique problems. Suffice it to say, the encoded themes communicated by patients seen under these conditions will be organized around the basic frame modifications inherent to the research. This is, simply, where the patient's deep unconscious perceptions and processing will be focused. In addition to interpreting the patient's material accordingly, every effort should be made to safeguard the patient's identity and to keep the clinical material in safe hands. Not infrequently, the interests and needs of the patient call for the termination of the recordings and the offer of a secured-frame, private therapy—conducted by the research therapist or through a referral to another therapist.

There is, however, no justifiable basis for presenting or publishing material from these patients' sessions. Recorded therapies are needed for quantitative research, but it is sufficient for publication purposes to present the measured data and results without revealing the actual material on which the research is based. An exception to this rule involves collaborators and other research teams for whom the raw data has importance. With respect to nonresearch publications, clinical material is merely illustrative, and because of selective and interpretive bias it cannot serve as valid evidence for or proof of clinical propositions. Fictitious vignettes, faithful to clinical experience, can be used to illustrate the points that an author is making; this is a basic secured-frame approach to this complex problem.

For those patients whose therapists unwisely do otherwise, the deviant qualities of the frame break are only compounded by involving the patient in the publication of his or her case material. In their need, unconsciously and maladaptively, to be abused and punished by their therapists, many patients are all too willing to play a role in the enactment of these frame violations. Such patients very much require frame-sensitive therapists to protect them from their pathological and self-hurtful, frame-deviant inclinations.

4.   Issues related to privacy and confidentiality are legion when it comes to clinic psychotherapies where violations of these ground rules are so common as to be truly alarming. Clinic frames are like sieves through which information about patients flows unobstructed and unsecured. There are many parties to and contexts for these deviations: secretaries and other clinic personnel who see and interact with patients and their records; presentations and discussions of intake sessions and case material; records and material released to other agencies and individuals; the presence of other patients, relatives of the patient, and strangers wandering through the clinic spaces; overheard conversations and observed records (the patients' own and those of other patients); and countless others violations of a similar kind.

There is a great need for clinic therapists to make gigantic efforts to minimize these intrusions and to try as best they can to secure more private and confidential therapeutic conditions for their clients. This includes establishing a policy of one therapist per patient and reducing to an essential minimum contacts with any inescapable third parties, including those who work in other agencies. As difficult as this may sound to the conscious mind, these frame breaks are having devastatingly harmful, deeply unconsciously mediated effects on clinic patients and their therapists. Unwittingly, they all too readily serve the self-destructive and maladaptive frame-deviant needs of all concerned. It is a situation in great need of repair.

> Ms Dory, a teenager, was in once-weekly psychotherapy with Dr Rice—a male therapist—because she suffered from anorexia nervosa. Her father paid for the therapy using his own cheques, which the patient brought to the sessions at the beginning of each new month to pay for the previous month's sessions.
>
> A year into the therapy, Dr Rice suffered a medical emergency that required minor surgery and would keep him from being in his office on the day of Ms Dory's session. He called the patient at home. Her father answered the telephone and told Dr Rice that his daughter was out. The therapist left a message

with the father that he'd be out of the office the next day and that he was cancelling Ms Dory's hour. He would see her the following week. With that, he ended the call.

Ms Dory began her session the following week by thanking the therapist for calling her; she hoped he was ok now. She then fell silent, and after a while said that she just didn't feel like talking. After another pause, she begrudgingly commented that she was upset by an incident that had happened at school earlier in the week. She had felt ill and had gone to the nurse's station at school, was given some aspirin, and then left school to go to the park and sit under a tree to rest a while. When her home-room teacher realized that she was not in school, she called her parents to report her absence.

Ms Dory, who was punished severely by her parents, was furious with her teacher. The teacher should have discussed this problem with her instead of her parents. She felt violated and betrayed; it felt as though the teacher had followed her home. She tried unsuccessfully to get her home-room teacher changed—she couldn't trust her any more. Ms Dory was afraid that if she made another mistake, the teacher would see to it that whole world would know about it.

Dr Rice interpreted this material as reflecting the patient's masochistic wish for punishment. The patient responded by again falling silent and then commenting that therapy seemed to be a waste of time.

Within a month of this incident, two further frame breaks occurred, both on the part of the patient. One was that she made a mistake in telling her father how many sessions had been held the previous month, and as a result she underpaid Dr Rice for the previous month's sessions. The other frame-break involved her missing a session to go to a movie with a girlfriend. When Dr Rice continued to pursue the fantasy basis for these actions, the patient became infuriated and quit therapy so that she could become a cheer leader.

As noted earlier, the ideal intervention with a single session cancellation is to not call the patient and to allow the patient to come to the office to discover the therapist's absence, thereby limiting the frame alteration to the therapist's missing the session. If this is intolerable for the therapist (and the problem is usually based on his or her own secured-frame anxieties), he or she may decide to call to inform the patient of the pending absence—a frame break with many risks to it.

For one, this information should be imparted to the patient alone—no third party should be involved. When this transpires, there are, nevertheless, frame modifications related to the time and place of contact between patient and therapist. Should a third party answer the telephone when the therapist calls, there is the added frame violation of the privacy of the therapy. Should the patient then be unavailable, even the therapist's limiting himself or herself to a good-bye creates a violation of the privacy of the treatment—a frame alteration that imposes a burden for the patient to work over in the following session, along with the deep unconscious realization that the therapist had an opportunity to hold the frame secured with regard to his or her absence and failed to do so.

The awkwardness of this type of frame modification is seen in the fact that the therapist would be further modifying the frame by asking the third party when the patient will be available to answer the telephone, yet calling back at another, randomly chosen time risks further third-party contact. It is for these reasons that simply missing such an hour is the most frame-securing intervention that the therapist can make and the most therapeutic choice for the patient. It is critical for therapists to analyse these situations in terms of deep unconscious rather than conscious standards and effects.

The derivatives in Ms Dory's story are quite unmistakable. The patient manifestly and consciously expressed gratitude for the therapist's frame-breaking telephone message. But she then encoded her unconscious perception of his call and revealed that she saw it as an infuriating betrayal, a violation of her right to privacy, and an invasive pursuit. The experience led her to mistrust the therapist and to think about leaving therapy—which she eventually did. She also proposed a rectification—these problems should be discussed with her and not her parents.

Dr Rice did not hear his patient's encoded messages. His interventions served to deny his betrayal of Ms Dory's right to privacy
for her therapy, and it held the patient accountable for his own
hurtful and harm-inviting deviant act. His failure to trigger decode and rectify the frame undoubtedly contributed to his
patient's frame-deviant acting out and premature termination of
the therapy—for both patient and therapist, modifying frames had
become a primary mode of adaptation. In a state of iatrogenic
paranoia, the patient unconsciously felt that the therapist's contact
with her father made it such that she no longer knew where, if
anywhere, the therapist would draw the line and not reveal her
secrets. She suffered from a profound sense of endangerment.

Finally, we may speculate that the uninterpreted deviant-
frame conditions of this therapy probably contributed to the
patient's decision to break the frame and leave school when she
felt ill. These conditions and the therapist's frame-breaking telephone call and conversation with Ms Dory's father appear to have
been factors in her error with the payment of the fee and her
missing a session for a frivolous reason. Frame deviations within a
psychotherapy prompt patients to break the frame both within
and outside treatment. They motivate patients to use frame breaking as a maladaptive and self-harmful mode of coping—all the
more so when the encoded messages from the patient's deep unconscious system are ignored.

Total privacy and total confidentiality are aspects of the secured frame that every patient deserves to have as basic conditions
for therapy. To hold the frame secured in these two vital areas is in
itself a major therapeutic achievement by a psychotherapist or
counsellor. It is deeply unconsciously appreciated and responded
to in constructive ways by all patients to whom this well-deserved,
healing gift is provided.

CHAPTER THIRTEEN

Neutrality and relative anonymity

In general, the more fluid and ill-defined a ground rule of psychotherapy, the greater the abuse of the rule. This helps to explain why, as measured by the standard of deep unconscious, encoded validation, violations of therapists' neutrality and relative anonymity are so common as to take on epidemic proportions. The pervasiveness of modifications of these two ground rules is also the result of the fact that, more than any other aspect of the frame, violation of these tenets extensively gratifies therapists' maladaptive needs for pathological forms of gratification at the expense of their patients. In all instances, these frame breaks introduce into a therapy the personally unresolved, unconscious pathological needs of the therapist, including his or her dread of secured frames. Such needs are, in their essence, inappropriate self-revelations of the first order. It therefore behoves us to take a careful and extended look at the nature and functions of these two ground rules and the issues raised by attempting to enforce their sound maintenance.

Problems of definition

There are many sources of the confusion and almost total disagreement among therapists as to the standards and properties of interventions that are called for by the ground rules of neutrality and relative anonymity. The meanings of both terms are derived primarily from loosely constructed theories and personal biases rather than empirical observations, and both tend to be ignored as important aspects of the secured frame.

In practice, the term *neutral* seems to be defined as any intervention accepted by a given theory of psychotherapy. Thus, interventions that are claimed to be neutral can range from the offer of directives and training exercises to those that are said to meet the impossible-to-define criteria of staying equidistant from the id, ego, superego, and reality. Similarly, the concept that therapists should be relatively anonymous to their patients is far from accepted in all quarters, while the *relative* aspect of anonymity is open to widely differing interpretations. In this regard, the range of possibilities runs from old-time psychoanalysts who hid themselves behind screens so as not to be seen by their patients, to the acceptance of therapists offering a wide range of personal opinions and information that are said to make the therapist more human and available to the patient.

Reflection indicates that the term *neutral* as applied to therapists' interventions is a misnomer because there is no such entity— every intervention made by a therapist has an impact. The concept of neutrality appears to have been developed to imply a lack of bias in the therapist, but no therapist is without theoretical and personal prejudice—some of it responsive to a patient's deeply unconscious therapeutic needs, some of it not.

The intended meaning of this ground rule seems best captured by defining neutrality in terms of some type of *validation* of therapists' interventions as reflected in patients' material and, secondarily, their behaviour. However, the exclusive use of a patient's behaviour or the alleviation of his or her symptoms are quite unreliable as sources for confirming the neutrality and helpfulness of an intervention because patients show many paradoxical, seemingly positive reactions to essentially harmful interventions. On the other hand, *communicative confirmation via positive and illuminating encoded (deep unconsciously derived) themes* has proven to be a reliable gauge of both neutrality and helpfulness—on the deep unconscious level, non-neutral interventions are consistently experienced as harmful and neutral identifications as curative. The defensiveness of the conscious system and of patients' manifest responses to interventions, as well as the inconsistency of conscious reactions, make it imperative to use *deep unconscious, encoded validation* as the criterion by which an intervention is judged to be neutral and healing. Encoded reactions to interventions are extremely consistent across individuals and offer sound evidence of the unconsciously experienced qualities of therapists' efforts—be they active comments, behaviour, or silences.

By this means, neutral interventions are defined as those efforts of a therapist that obtain encoded confirmation via the emergence of positive themes of well-functioning and wise individuals (*interpersonal validation*) and themes that add significant understanding to a therapist's prior comment or action (*cognitive validation*; see Langs, 1982, 1992). These criteria apply to all extended silences, active comments, behaviour, and framing efforts made by therapists. *Non-neutral interventions* are those that fail to obtain this affirming communicative response. *Non-validation* is reflected in patients' responsive material that lacks confirmatory images and in themes of bias, errors, lack of understanding, blindness and deafness, exploitation, harm, seduction, and the like.

These criteria apply to all types of interventions by therapists working in all manner of ways on the basis of varying theoretical underpinnings. It does of course set the standard of *deep unconscious validation* as the basic means of ensuring a therapist's neutrality and, by implication, his or her doing proper and constructive work with psychotherapy patients. It is, as well, based on the claim that deep unconscious experience is the most critical factor in emotional life and its healthy and dysfunctional moments—and in the healing aspects of a psychotherapy experience.

Similar considerations apply to the definition of *relative anonymity*. Conscious system responses, as reflected in the manifest contents and the implications of patients' direct themes, are not trustworthy as a means of assessing the validity of interventions involving revelations pertaining to the personal life and opinions of the therapist (see below). Indeed, patients consciously tolerate and accept a wide range of self-revelations from their therapists, some of them blatantly damaging on the surface and all of them damaging at the deeply unconsciously level. Thus, here too a patients' *deep unconscious, encoded responses* provide the only reliable basis for judging the effects of these personal disclosures by therapists. With great consistency, patients' encoded themes indicate that all such revelations are indeed frame violations with harmful consequences.

Unconsciously validated interventions

The term *neutral intervention* is intended to define those efforts of psychotherapists that are deeply helpful to patients. Its definition should provide standards through which therapists can ensure their use of optimal interventions and avoid being harmful to their patients and disruptive to their therapies. It is, then, a prime safeguard against a therapist's acting out of his or her counter-transference-based needs.

Using the criterion of encoded validation, there are only two classes of intervention that consistently prove to be neutral. They are:

1. *Interpretations based on trigger decoding a patient's narrative material*

Clinical studies have clearly shown that there is only one class of verbal interventions by psychotherapists that obtain encoded confirmation. This finding tends to be quite surprising to therapists who have been conducting their psychotherapies in terms of manifest contents and their implications. These therapists make use of a wide variety of interventions, which, on the surface, are accepted by patients and seem to "move things along". But the failure to decode the encoded meanings of patients' material as they respond to these interventions has led them to miss the harmful qualities of such work. Patients are under inner pressures to adapt to the traumas created by their therapists, and they do so by communicating narrative material that seems interesting on the surface but contains strong condemnations of their therapists on the encoded level.

The type of intervention that is validated by the deep unconscious system is one that is based on the realization that conscious adaptation and, especially, deep unconscious adaptation to emotionally charged events are the primary functions of the emotion-processing mind. Thus, the intervention begins with the identification of an activating triggering event for the patient's communications—most often a framing action by the therapist. It then shifts to the patient's encoded images, organizing and decoding their themes as the patient's selected unconscious perceptions of the actual meanings of what the therapist has said or done.

When the material permits, the ideal intervention will then include an understanding of the fantasies and memories activated by the trigger. The relevant genetic connections are defined as references to earlier life experiences that have been recalled because in some fashion the present intervention by the therapist bears a psychological similarity to those past events. If the patient has included encoded suggestions as to how to set the situation straight—encoded correctives or models of rectification—these are both interpreted and actually used as guidelines for further interventions, as when they direct the therapist to secure an aspect of the frame. The intervention usually concludes with a demonstration of how the entire activated experience and its selected meanings are the deep unconscious basis for the patient's emotional dysfunctions—*his or her symptomatic and/or resistance patient-indicators.*

This translates into the following model interpretation:

"I [the therapist] did this or that—you [the patient] unconsciously experienced it in that or this way—and what I [the therapist] said or did recalled and repeated in some way this or that past event in your [the patient's] life. All of this is related unconsciously to this or that problem that you've [the patient] been having. And, finally, you're suggesting that in the future I do thus and thus [i.e. rectify a frame deviation]."

It is well to understand that while the conscious system will, on the surface, accept virtually anything that a therapist says and does, the deep unconscious system is very strict and narrow in its criteria of *acceptable and truly helpful* interventions by therapists. The lack of familiarity with how the deep unconscious system perceives, operates, and copes makes its position seem strange and rigid to the conscious mind. In reality, however, patients' deep unconscious systems are simply trying to inform us as therapists that there are very few interventions that are genuinely helpful to them as patients, and that we should, if at all possible, learn what they are and use them exclusively.

The criteria of valid interventions presented here also reflects another distinctive attribute of the deep unconscious system. It is a system focused on immediate experience and on the frame qualities of impacting events. Intervening along other lines may make sense consciously and may illuminate manifest issues, but nevertheless such comments will be experienced deeply unconsciously as erroneous, as hurtful, and as a way of avoiding more compelling and disturbing issues and meanings related to the framing of the psychotherapy. Using conscious system criteria of confirmation, psychotherapists tend to work in areas of emotional life that are relatively trivial and unempowered. Using deep unconscious system criteria, they work where the strength of emotional life and psychotherapy reside.

In order to intervene validly, then, a therapist needs two elements: (1) a manifest allusion to a frame-related triggering event; (2) powerful encoded derivative material. In sessions in which the derivatives are strong and deeply meaningful, but the frame-related trigger is not referred to directly, the therapist may intervene if there is a general bridge or reference to the therapy or therapist. Under these conditions, the therapist can offer a playback of the strongest encoded themes organized around the unmentioned triggering event—a partial interpretation in the form of a *playback of derivatives*. The playback begins with the bridge to therapy, alludes next to the best encoded representation of the trigger, and then plays back to the patient his or her encoded perceptions of the unmentioned, frame-related triggering event (see chapter four; see also Langs, 1992).

Validation of this type of interpretation usually takes the form of the patient's direct recall of the missing trigger. However, when the trigger is especially anxiety provoking, validation may be restricted to the encoded level and take the form of the addition of fresh derivatives that further illuminate the deep unconscious meanings of the repressed trigger. In all, trigger-decoded interpretations and trigger-organized playbacks of derivatives are the only interventions that obtain encoded validation from patients.

2.   *Interventions involved in managing the ground rules of a psychotherapy, which in principle entails securing the frame at the behest of the patient's derivative messages*

Patients' encoded themes in response to a therapists' frame-management efforts will validate only those interventions that secure the frame. Modifications or departures from the unconsciously sought, ideal frame will not obtain encoded confirmation and will, instead, evoke themes of mismanagement, misunderstanding, seduction, harm, and the like.

* * *

Correct trigger-decoded, frame-related interpretations and efforts to hold or secure the ground rules of psychotherapy are the only two classes of interventions that obtain encoded validation. At times, an interpretation of a patient's unconscious perception of a therapist's missed intervention will also obtain encoded confirmation. However, in these cases, the material will return to the working over of the frame-related triggering event that the therapist has overlooked in making the erroneous intervention. Eventually, the patient's unconscious experience of this earlier frame-related trigger must be interpreted—and rectified, if needed—by the therapist.

With the type of interventions that obtain encoded validation so restricted, what can be said of the many other types of interventions that have been used and advocated through the years by various schools of psychotherapy, including psychoanalysis? The answer is simple but disquieting: they are not neutral, they do not obtain encoded validation, and they do not have favourable deep unconscious effects on patients.

There are several reasons for the non-validation of interventions in the form of questions, clarifications, confrontations, isolated reconstructions, suggestions, directives, personal opinions, and the like. These interventions are used by therapists who do not understand or work with the encoded meanings of their patients' material. Thus, these non-interpretive efforts are correctly *perceived unconsciously* by patients as failures to trigger decode and as attempts by therapists to interrupt and avoid patients' deep unconscious perceptions of their therapists' errors and their harmful ramifications. Unconsciously, these interventions are validly seen by patients as reflections of the countertransferences and counter-resistances of the therapist. Almost always, these manifestly oriented interventions are made in place of trigger-decoded interpretations. Thus, patients deeply unconsciously experience therapists who use these interventions as attempting to take flight from deeper and more powerful meanings that, at their core, pertain to the therapist on the basis of his or her most recent frame-related interventions.

A good rule to follow is that *in each session, the patient should be allowed to create the interpretations and frame-management efforts of the therapist*. When the patient needs to resist communicatively and not provide the therapist with the ingredients for intervening—a manifest representation of an active frame-related trigger and strong encoded themes—the therapist should respect the communicative resistance and not attempt to override it. The effort should be made to understand the triggers (i.e. interventions) that are contributing to the resistance—*all resistances are interactionally cast*. When the patient unconsciously experiences an emotional need for an intervention—by evolved design, emotion-processing minds are unable to develop most deep unconscious insights (correct links between triggers and themes) on their own—the elements necessary for intervening will be offered in his or her material, and the therapist will be in a position to make the interpretation and frame-management response that the patient needs.

The attributes of relative anonymity

The ground rule that calls for the *relative anonymity* of the psychotherapist exists as a safeguard against the therapist's imposing his or her issues, needs, conflicts, defences, psychopathology, maladaptive preferences, and other countertransferences onto the patient. Given that the patient is continually introjecting aspects of the therapist's functioning, needs, defences, and other psychological attributes, interventions that violate the therapist's relative anonymity create destructive introjects and subject the patient to pathological pressures that disturb the therapeutic process. Inherently, all breaks in relative anonymity unconsciously also place the therapist in the role of patient and ask the patient to assume the role of the therapist. Harm is thereby suffered by the patient, and the therapist will suffer from conscious and especially unconscious guilt.

The essential definition of relative anonymity limits what a therapist reveals about himself or herself to those aspects of his or her adaptations, personality, behaviour, and self that constitute an inescapable minimum. This precept does not imply a sterilization of the therapist's approach to and interaction with the patient. It simply indicates that, while the therapist should adopt a natural and professional demeanor in his or her therapeutic work, deliberate self-revelations and off-hand comments are detrimental to the healing goals of psychotherapy and may cause considerable psychological damage to the patient.

The therapist's office-setting and decor, style of dress, manner of speaking, and many attributes of his or her successes and failures in intervening are the kinds of features that inescapably are conveyed to patients—both consciously and unconsciously. Beyond these qualities, however, there is much that a therapist might reveal in a social setting that is curtailed in the psychotherapy situation. This is done because of the definitive role assignment of the therapist and the strictures that this places on him or her in the service of the therapeutic needs of the patient, which are the primary guiding force of the treatment situation.

This precept implies, then, that a therapist's personal history, current private life-circumstances, beliefs, accomplishments, opinions, needs, and the like are not conveyed to patients. Indeed, the therapist's communications and behaviour should be based entirely on the patient's material in a given session and restricted to the necessities of effecting deep unconsciously validated, healing therapeutic work. Violation of this ground rule is both a technical error and a revelation of aspects of the therapist's emotional difficulties—they impose a considerable burden on the patient.

There is a natural tendency and need among therapists as human beings to modify the rule of relative anonymity. The emotion-processing mind has evolved with defensive needs and pathological self-gratifications as strong motivating forces. The rule of relative anonymity—as is true of all of the ground rules—requires that therapists work through, resolve, and renounce these ultimately destructive inclinations.

Therapists should find the means of satisfying the more healthy aspects of their emotional needs in their private lives. The personally (and professionally) satisfied therapist is far more likely to adhere to the ideal ground rules of psychotherapy than one who is frustrated and unhappy in his or her personal life. But regardless of the status of a therapist's outside life, his or her commitment to the patient calls for strict adherence to the ground rule of relative anonymity.

A patient's deep unconscious mind is exceedingly sensitive to the least violation of this canon, and the repercussions of a lapse can be extensive—especially if the therapist fails to realize that he or she has committed a frame break. On the other hand, if the therapist recognizes an inadvertent violation in relative anonymity, he or she is in a position to decode and interpret the patient's responsive disguised narratives and to rectify the frame-break to the greatest extent feasible. This kind of interlude is therefore both hurtful and reparative—a not uncommon happening in the most sound psychotherapy experience.

It must be acknowledged, however, that many violations of relative anonymity—that is, self-revelations, information about a therapist's family members, stated religious preferences, and so forth—cannot be undone and fully rectified. The residual effects of these frame violations may endure throughout a therapy and be somewhat damaging regardless of the amount of sound therapeutic work done around the deviant intervention. We are reminded that nature is nature, and that the consequences of many traumas cannot be fully repaired.

Ms Janis, a woman in her early 30s, was in psychotherapy with Dr Parker because of a severe depression suffered after her fiancé broke their engagement. Towards the end of the first year of her therapy, Dr Parker called Ms Janis one evening at her apartment to cancel her next session. He simply said that he wouldn't be in his office and had to cancel her session, and the patient said that she hoped everything was all right and added that she would see him the following week.

In the next session, the patient told a story about her girlfriend, Ellen, who was in bed one evening when she heard a noise at her door and realized that someone was trying to break into her apartment. She screamed hysterically and evidently frightened off the intruder, whom she could hear running away. Ms Janis opined that no one is safe in this city any more, not even in their own apartment.

Her thoughts shifted to a newspaper story in which a woman was raped in her apartment by a man who got in through an open window. It wasn't the first time a rape had occurred in that apartment building. Ms Janis concluded that men can't be trusted, and she went on to detail several unpleasant experiences that she had suffered with insensitive men, including her fiancé who had become involved with another woman and had deserted her.

Dr Parker intervened and pointed out that Ms Janis had been hurt badly by what her fiancé had done. As a result, her view of men seemed jaundiced and maybe even a bit biased and unfair. It seemed also that there was an unconscious fantasy that he, Dr Parker, too was not to be trusted, because he was a man. This also must have to do with her father, who was unfaithful to her mother. It would be well for Ms Janis to think about why she chooses men like her father and how her unconscious view of men makes it impossible for her to recognize when a man is faithful to her—himself included.

Ms Janis felt annoyed with Dr Parker and responded by saying that he seemed to be a man defending men. Dr Parker suggested that she was resisting his interpretation and not giving it any thought. The patient sighed and said that she really had no idea of what she does and why she does it—it's hard to admit that you don't know yourself. Her fiancé was like that, always thinking that he was right and she was wrong. She should have known he was trouble. After their engagement, he broke a date one night, saying he had to work late at the office. But then her girlfriend saw him in a restaurant with another woman. When Ms Janis confronted him with this fact, he attacked her for not trusting him—talk about crazy defences. He wouldn't listen to her when she tried to get to him to set things right. She should have broken the engagement then instead of waiting around for more abuse and hurt. He had no idea how insensitive he'd been. She wished Dr Parker hadn't cancelled her session last week; she'd been severely depressed for ten days and needed to see him.

Dr Parker intervened again. He pointed out that Ms Janis had mentioned his cancelling her session. He had intervened earlier about her jaundiced view of men and she had responded by talking about men who don't understand how hurtful they have been. It seems that she has been working over the cancellation, and he evidently had not understood that this was the case. Her earlier images were about men breaking into women's apartments and raping them. He had called her at her apartment, so it seems that the call was experienced by her as an assault, a rape. There also was the story of her fiancé breaking a date with her to be with another woman, which must be how she experienced his cancelling her hour.

Ms Janis admitted that she had been shocked to hear her therapist's voice when she answered the telephone. She had had the weird thought at first that he was calling her for a date. This reminded her of another telephone call she had received a year earlier. It was to inform her that a short story she had written had won a prize, so not every phone call needs to be bad news. It also occurred to her that, strangely enough, when her father left her mother, he told her about it over the telephone rather than face-to-face with her. She—Ms Janis—must have felt abandoned when Dr Parker called to tell her she would not have a session last week.

Dr Parker apologized for calling her at home. He felt he should explain why he did what he did. His wife needed emergency surgery for a bowel obstruction, which is why everything had happened so unexpectedly. He hoped that this would help Ms Janis better understand the incident.

Ms Janis got angry again and felt that Dr Parker was making excuses. She was sorry to hear about his wife, but that brought up surgery and surgeons, and she didn't want to hear about any of that. She recalled a visit to a surgeon two years earlier because she had felt some nodules in her breast. He began to fondle her breasts, complaining that his wife was frigid and saying that Ms Janis was a very attractive woman. She ran like hell from his office, and to this day she's sorry she didn't report him to the medical licensing board.

Dr Parker is a therapist with a sense of deep unconscious communication, but he is mainly committed to a classical psychodynamic way of thinking. His absence from Ms Janis' session ideally should have occurred without his notifying her. His decision to make the call was frame-deviant, but it would have been workable had he understood her encoded, deep unconscious response to the frame break. Instead, he initially made a classically oriented interpretation of the patient's supposedly distorted unconscious view of men and of himself in the so-called transference.

Notice that Dr Parker introduced material into his intervention that the patient had not produced in the session at hand. This is a not uncommon practice of psychotherapists, and it reflects conscious system tendencies. However, these arbitrary interventions do not obtain encoded validation and are technically non-neutral and erroneous. They are seen deeply unconsciously as intrusive and as self-revealing, as well as being a violation of therapists' relative anonymity because their selection of additional comments reflect their own unconscious needs rather than those of their patients. Clinical studies indicate that these addenda almost always reflect therapists' countertransferences rather than helpful supplements.

Given that the material from the session encoded the patient's deep unconscious perceptions of the therapist's frame break and reflected a valid appreciation for selected aspects of its unconscious meanings, we can see that the intervention stands reality on its head: a valid, unconscious perception of the therapist's intrusion is misinterpreted as a genetically driven, invalid, or distorted fantasy. The intervention also denies the existence of the hurtful frame break that the therapist had made and holds the patient accountable for a pathological position when it was the therapist who had behaved in a frame-deviant, pathological manner.

The patient's response to the therapist's first intervention is a good example of non-validation. The themes stress a lack of understanding and of self-insight, and speak of insisting on being right when you are wrong. The story about the fiancé's abandonment and betrayal encodes the patient's unconscious perceptions of the therapist's immediate intervention, which abandons the patient at her time of need. In addition, through condensation, it also encodes the patient's view of the cancelled session.

When the patient alluded directly to this triggering event, Dr Parker apparently realized that his prior intervention had been in error—that he had not understood how the cancellation of the patient's hour was serving as the trigger and organizer of Ms Janis' narrative themes and their encoded meanings. He then offered the patient a sound interpretation of her encoded perceptions of the triggering event and obtained strong encoded validation in the story of the telephone call that announced that she had earned a prize—her talent as a writer encoded her therapist's talent as a therapist. She then added a genetic link to the situation in that the therapist's call and cancellation had repeated in some form the telephone call that her mother had received from her father to announce his abandonment of his family.

But at this juncture Dr Parker lost his position of both neutrality and relative anonymity. He revealed the personal reason for his call, and the patient reacted sharply with strong and clear, negative derivatives. The therapist's self-revelation was experienced deeply unconsciously as an attempt at sexual seduction tantamount to malpractice. This was, for Ms Janis, as it would be for any patient, a devastating frame break. We may speculate that the existential death anxieties evoked by his wife's illness played a significant role in Dr Parker's sudden violation of the frame of this therapy.

This vignette also offers an opportunity to compare the selections of deep unconscious meaning shown by three different patients with different therapists in responding to similar frame violations—Ms Janis and Mr York in chapter ten, and Ms Dory in chapter twelve. Based on her personal life history and therapy experiences, Ms Janis' deep unconscious selections stressed the seductive and rapacious aspects of the therapist's intrusion. On the other hand, Mr York experienced his therapist's call to him at work as a dangerous, psychotic intrusion, while Ms Dory emphasized both intrusion and betrayal (this latter in part because of the therapist's frame-breaking contact with her father). This comparison illustrates how patient's respond to comparable triggers with a personal selection of relevant meanings taken from the universal attributes of an intervention—here, a modification of the frame.

Finally, we may note again that the ideal ground rules of psychotherapy are not a set of arbitrary, rigid, outdated canons, but are instead a carefully honed, deeply unconsciously validated set of precepts whose most important goals are to protect the patient—and therapist—from harm and error, and to create the conditions under which sound cure can be achieved.

CHAPTER FOURTEEN

Issues in
managing the frame

In this final chapter, I present some over-arching precepts regarding the management of the ground rules of psychotherapy and touch on some of the more pressing unresolved issues related to this critical aspect of treatment. My themes are both practical and theoretical, and they are developed as a way of rounding out our insights into this most telling aspect of human and therapeutic experience.

The hierarchy of frame issues

Given the many and diverse components of the ground rules of psychotherapy and the central role that they play in organizing the deep unconscious experiences of both patients and therapists, sessions in which there is but a single active frame issue are exceedingly rare. Often enough, a recent frame-securing or frame-modifying intervention will dominate the picture, but in many instances there are two or more equally compelling frame issues with which a patient is dealing. This leads us to ask whether there is a general hierarchy of frame-related, adaptation-evoking triggers that assigns an order of general precedence to each type of frame issue. In addition, can we establish some basic principles of technique for handling multiple, simultaneous frame impingements?

As to the first question, there is indeed a hierarchy of frame impingements. Some of the main guidelines are:

1. *When both basic types of framing events occur, frame-modifying interventions take precedence over frame-securing interventions.* On occasions where a therapist secures a deviant aspect of the ground rules, but also breaks the frame in some other fashion, the frame-modifying intervention will keep the frame essentially in a deviant state. This lessens the impact of the frame-securing effort and renders the patient's deep unconscious responses to the frame-deviant intervention the more important to interpret and rectify if possible—after which the activated secured-frame anxieties and issues will merit interpretation.

2. *Unnecessary frame modifications take precedence over those that are an inherent part of the therapeutic situation.* In clinic situations or when, for example, insurance coverage is part of a private psychotherapy, an additional and unnecessary frame deviation by the therapist will have more power than the deviations built into the therapy. The latter still have their harmful effects, but the patient's derivatives and the therapeutic work are likely, for the moment, to be more focused on the unneeded deviation than on the in-built ones. In addition, however, the acute frame violation will prompt a patient's secondary working over of the basic flaws in the therapy frame.

3. *Current frame-related interventions take precedence over those from the past.* As a rule, past frame deviations are activated by current frame deviations, past frame-securing moments by current frame-securing moments. It is therefore essential for a therapist to identify and work with a patient's reaction to a currently active frame-related intervention before exploring re-activated aspects of past framing efforts. In the deep unconscious system, the present takes precedence over—yet re-activates—the past.

4. *The therapist's frame-related interventions take precedence over the patient's frame-related behaviour.* In principle, patients' efforts to modify the frame are motivated by both their own unconscious needs and prior frame modifications by their therapists. It is the therapist who has the primary responsibility for establishing and maintaining the ground rules of therapy—the patient's obligations are secondary, though also critical. It follows, then, that the therapist's efforts in this area have more power and greater importance than those of the patient.

An exception to this rule arises when a patient wishes to modify the frame severely, as with a sudden decision to terminate a therapy prematurely. This frame modification must be used to organize the patient's material in terms of his or her self-perceptions related to the proposed frame break. The patient's narrative themes will reveal his or her deep unconscious perceptions of this pending action, but they will also indicate the critical frame-related triggers, usually frame modifying, that have prompted the patient's deviant intentions. Thus, the interpretative work with this *resistance patient-indicator* is incomplete and is not likely to enable the patient to remain insightfully in therapy, without the discovery through the patient's material of the adaptation-evoking triggers that have motivated the patient to create this type of emergency situation.

5. *A deliberate and knowing frame modification takes precedence over an accidental or inadvertent one.* All other things being equal, frame breaks that stem from a therapist's ignorance of the ideal ground rules or that occur accidentally—as when a therapist inadvertently locks a patient out of the office—have somewhat less power than those breaks that are done with the conscious awareness that the frame is being modified.

6. *Frame modifications by therapists themselves take precedence over third-party frame violations.* While therapists are held responsible for third-party deviations such as a personal revelation about the therapist by one of his or her friends, these third-party frame breaks are, in principle, less powerful than similar deviations made by the therapist himself or herself. However, because third-party deviations tend to involve violations of the

therapist's relative anonymity and often entail the revelation of highly charged aspects of the therapist's personal life, these other-person deviations nevertheless tend to have strong effects.

7. *The more personal the deviation, the greater its power.* For example, a therapist's lateness to session will have less power than a revelation that someone in his or her family is ill.

These hierarchical layers are complex, and there is usually a combination of factors determining which of several active frame-breaking triggers a given patient will react to most strongly. The nature of the frame violation, the vicissitudes of the patient's life history, and the status of his or her current mental status are factors in this selection process.

Clinically, in the presence of multiple frame modifications, a patient will *unconsciously select* a particular infringement for working over and active adaptation. His or her derivative themes will organize primarily around the particular framing intervention of greatest importance to him or her—although these themes will, secondarily, organize—through condensation—around the other active frame deviations as well.

In many cases, it proves to be impossible—even for a therapist who uses his or her knowledge of the above-mentioned hierarchies—to predict which frame break the patient will work over most strongly at a given moment. Also, the patient usually has no conscious idea why his or her unconscious selection has been made. This discrepancy between conscious and deep unconscious concerns and focus reflects the relative independence of the operations of the conscious and deep unconscious systems of the emotion-processing mind.

This finding enables us to develop a key principle of technique in dealing with multiple frame modifications. The therapist should *not* try to select the frame break that is to be interpreted to, and managed with, the patient. The patient must be allowed to make that choice unconsciously. It has to be emphasized that this selection process must be made *unconsciously rather than consciously*— that is, a patient's directly announced frame concern is likely to be defensively chosen and probably not the prime issue for his or her deep unconscious system. The conscious system tends to choose to work over the less powerful of two active triggers. Thus, patients generally try to link their available themes to a weaker rather than stronger trigger, doing so in ways that are forced and awkward because the themes fit better with and more incisively illuminate the more powerful triggering event. The therapist must therefore be guided by the patient's encoded themes rather than by his or her own—or the patient's—conscious choices. A helpful clue to the key frame issue is the ways in which the power themes represent and flow into and elucidate a particular triggering event.

Making frame-related choices

There are several types of frame-related choices that therapists are called upon to make from time to time in the course of a psychotherapy. With the possible exception of dire emergencies involving matters of life and death, when the therapist's choice is between holding the frame secured or deviating—the preferred response should always be that of *keeping the frame secured*. But there are, as well, many situations in which the therapist is in a position where he or she has no choice but to modify the frame one way or another. In these circumstances, the key principle states that *the choice should always be that of the least disruptive and least deviant frame modification*.

As an example, consider a situation where a decision has to be made whether to hold the frame secured or modify a ground rule: a patient calls her therapist and leaves a message on his answering machine, asking for a change in the time of her session that week. The choice facing the therapist is between compounding the patient's frame break with a deviation of his own by returning the call, or holding the frame secured by not calling the patient back.

The patient has modified the ideal frame both by making the telephone call (this is an attempt to make deviant contact with the therapist outside the time of their appointments, and at a time when the patient is not in the therapist's office) and by asking for the change to the time of the session (a violation of the set time and day for the sessions). The therapist would also be modifying the frame by returning the call (another violation of the set locale and time for contact between patient and therapist). In addition, if the therapist decided not to offer a different time for the patient's session, he would have first modified the frame and then secured it. If he chose to offer an alternative hour, he would be modifying the frame in two ways—by returning the call and changing the time of the session. Clearly, not returning the call is the frame-securing solution—any other choice would be frame-deviant.

Whatever the therapist's decision, the session that follows will find the patient dealing deeply unconsciously with her own frame break and the therapist's framing response. The patient's violation of the ideal ground rules is *a frame-related patient-indicator* that calls for the discovery of the framing trigger that has evoked it and for suitable trigger-decoded interpretations of its meanings—and rectification if the trigger is frame-deviant and correctable.

The situation is quite different when, for example, a patient seeing a male therapist leaves her suit jacket on a chair as she is leaving her session. Here, the therapist's two choices are both frame deviant: on the one hand, he may choose to say nothing and thereby deviate by holding on to a part of the patient for the intervening week; on the other hand, he may decide to say something to the patient about the jacket, thereby breaking the frame by speaking to her after the session is at an end.

In *assessing the frame qualities* of these two possible interventions, we see that both interventions break the frame in order to secure it. In this light, the therapist's choice should be based on which action is least deviant and most frame securing. In this case, speaking to the patient after the end of the session is far less deviant than keeping her jacket (unconsciously experienced as part of the patient) in his office for a week—a decision that would, of necessity, compound the deviation by having to touch the jacket as well. In the following hour, the choice that the therapist has made will be a prime trigger for the patient's encoded material, but, in addition, a search must be made for the trigger that had evoked the patient's frame-deviant action in the first place.

In principle, breaking the frame in order to secure it is to be preferred to simply breaking the frame, although securing the frame is best of all.

These kinds of choices are not uncommon. The least deviant and most secured selections should prevail, but sorting out the possibilities in just a few available seconds is not easy—largely because the conscious system of the emotion-processing mind is deviant-prone. What is required of therapists is a *secured-frame attitude and value system* that will facilitate making the best frame-securing response almost intuitively.

Transfers from clinic settings to private practice

In chapter nine, I discussed some of the distinctive and difficult attributes of psychotherapy undertaken in clinics and other agencies. The deviant setting and modified ground rules of these forms of therapy create all sorts of problems for both patients and therapists. Quite often, this kind of therapy culminates in an announcement by the therapist that he or she will soon be leaving the clinic. Whether this occurs because the therapist is a trainee or because he or she has decided to work elsewhere, this triggering event is extremely traumatic for the patient—and the therapist as well. It is a crucial adaptation-evoking stimulus that the patient is compelled to deal with both consciously and unconsciously until the end of the therapy with that therapist—and long after as well.

If the therapist is initiating or has an on-going private practice, the question arises as to whether it is best for the patient frame-wise, and with respect to his or her therapeutic needs, to remain at the clinic and continue the therapy with a new therapist (who may well repeat the same desertion trauma) or move with the present therapist to his or her private office.

This is another example of a situation in which a therapist must choose between two essentially frame-modifying interventions. Leaving the patient before his or her therapy has been completed violates the ground rule that commits the therapist to see the patient through to a suitable patient-determined termination. But taking a patient from a clinic to a therapist's private office modifies several ground rules—the commitment see the patient in the clinic setting; possibly, the set time for sessions; and probably the rule of a single, set fee for the therapy.

Even manifestly, the frame break of taking the patient into private therapy has seductive and exploitative features, and it is often automatically favoured by therapists who are starting out in private practice. In making the move, there also is the possible added deviation of charging the patient a very low fee for the private therapy, one that appears consciously and/or deeply unconsciously to be a self-sacrificing act by the therapist. The deep unconscious ramifications of the change from a clinic to a private setting extend from these surface considerations into incisive deep unconscious perceptions of the therapist's deviant needs. Still, the transfer to the private office undoes the therapist's abandonment of the patient and usually offers the patient a far more secured setting and set of ground rules than those that prevail at the clinic—the move does have its frame-securing aspects.

Clinical experience indicates that, in most cases, continuing with the same therapist in his or her private office is the least harmful choice for the patient. Leaving the patient in the clinic truly exposes him or her to the likelihood of additional abandonments by future therapists and keeps the patient in a basically frame-deviant setting in which he or she is at great risk. The transfer to a private office secures many aspects of the therapy frame that are modified in the clinic situation. In most cases, then, the move offers the patient a dramatic frame-securing moment with the potential for considerable therapeutic gain. The patient's secured-frame anxieties are activated and the underlying issues become available for therapeutic work, and the prevailing frame deviations prove to be somewhat workable because of the secured aspects of the new framework of the therapy.

A patient's secured-frame anxieties tend to increase markedly with the shift to a private setting. Considerable therapeutic work must be done to enable the patient to stay in and benefit from his or her new secured-frame therapy situation. Indeed, the change in setting reveals the extent of most patients' deep unconscious investment in the deviant-frame qualities of clinic settings. The highly defensive, communication-limiting, frame-modifying mode of adaptation reinforced by clinic settings and clinic therapists suits patients' pathological needs and protects them from secured-frame, death-related anxieties. However, as noted, these are the very anxieties that must be worked through if a patient is to have a sound and lasting cure.

Cure through secured-frame holding

Finally, we should recognize a group of patients for whom a therapist's holding to the ideal ground rules of psychotherapy does most of the emotional healing. These patients characteristically are quite schizoid or have a history of relatively brief hospitalizations for borderline or ambulatory schizophrenic problems. There are indications of severe psychopathology and a primitive inner mental world, reflected at times in bizarre thoughts, behaviour, and/or dreams.

These patients tend to accept the ideal frame when it is offered to them, especially if they have been traumatized by deviant-frame therapists in the past. They quickly settle into once- or twice-weekly therapy without challenging or modifying the frame. There are, then, few active frame-related triggers for these patients to deal with, and their material becomes derivative-poor, with few power themes—though appropriately so. The patient makes no effort to modify the frame unilaterally, nor does he or she attempt to evoke frame modifications by the therapist. The therapist therefore has little, if any, cause to intervene actively for long periods of time. Holding the frame secured and not disturbing the situation is his or her main contribution to the patient's cure.

Such patients appear to have had major life traumas, and their inner mental worlds and mode of deep unconscious experience are exceedingly primitive, raw, and terrifying. Unconsciously, they attempt to avoid encoded expressions, because they are frightened of the activation of the death anxieties and the terrible unconscious perceptions and memories that they would experience were they to do so. As a result, their cure transpires when the therapist wisely remains silent and effectively holds the patient secure—and continues to do so unless a frame issue and a few encoded derivatives emerge. The absence of errors in intervening and the holding of the frame secured provides the patient with a safe setting and positive introject of the soundly intervening therapist that allows for quiet self-healing without the process being disrupted by intrusive interventions and primitive conscious and unconscious experiences that are difficult to master.

As is true of all patients, when these patients need a trigger-decoded interpretation from their therapists, they will modify—or try to get the therapist to modify—an aspect of the ground rules. This should prompt the therapist to hold the frame secured and to discover a prior trigger that has activated the patient's assault on the frame—possibly a minor deviant lapse or an active frame-securing moment. Interpretation of the *frame-altering patient-indicator* is then feasible, and validation often includes the recall of an illuminating genetic event that connects the present situation to past traumas. Once this work is absorbed by the patient, he or she will again settle back into the non-derivative mode, and the therapist's holding will once more take over as the curative factor in the therapy.

Concluding comments

I have tried in this book to offer a comprehensive exploration of the extensive ramifications, many of them not as yet fully appreciated, of a therapist's establishing and managing the ground rules of psychotherapy. Simply put, properly managing the framework and ground rules of therapy and counselling is perhaps the most salient and powerful responsibility that a therapist has to his or her patients in their search for effective, non-symptomatic emotional adaptations. Dealing with rules, frames, and boundaries is a facet of both psychotherapy and everyday life for which humans have, for reasons of anxiety and defence, evolved natural maladaptive conscious preferences. Thus, the mastery of this dimension of human experience and behaviour, within and outside of therapy, is one of the most satisfying and health-giving goals that a psychotherapist can pursue—both they and their patients stand to benefit enormously from the success of this great and marvellous pursuit.

REFERENCES

Bickerton, D. (1990). *Language and Species*. Chicago, IL: University of Chicago Press.

Bollas, C., & Sundelson, D. (1996). *The New Informants: The Betrayal of Confidentiality in Psychoanalysis and Psychotherapy*. Northvale, NJ: Jason Aronson.

Corballis, C. (1991). *The Lopsided Ape*. New York: Oxford University Press.

deDuve, C. (1995). *Vital Dust*. New York: Basic Books.

Dennett, D. (1996). *Kinds of Minds*. New York: Basic Books.

Freud, S. (1912). Recommendations to physicians practicing psycho-analysis. *Standard Edition, Vol. 12* (pp. 109–120).

Freud, S. (1913). On beginning treatment (further recommendations on the technique of psycho-analysis). *Standard Edition, Vol 12* (pp. 121–144).

Gabbard, G., & Lester, E. (1995). *Boundaries and Boundary Violations*. New York: Basic Books.

Goleman, D. (1995). *Emotional Intelligence*. New York: Bantam.

Haskell, R. (1991). An analogical methodology for the analysis and validation of anomalous cognitive and linguistic operations in small group (fantasy theme) reports. *Small Group Research*, 22: 443–474.

Hogenson, G. (1994 [1983]). *Jung's Struggle with Freud*. Wilmette, IL: Chiron.

Langs, R. (1976). *The Therapeutic Interaction, Vols. 1 & 2*. Northvale, NJ: Jason Aronson.

Langs, R. (1979). *The Therapeutic Environment*. Northvale, NJ: Jason Aronson.

Langs, R. (1982). *Psychotherapy: A Basic Text*. Northvale, NJ: Jason Aronson.

Langs, R. (1992). *A Clinical Workbook for Psychotherapists*. London: Karnac Books.

Langs, R. (1993). *Empowered Psychotherapy*. London: Karnac Books.

Langs, R. (1994). *Doing Supervision and Being Supervised*. London: Karnac Books.

Langs, R. (1995). *Clinical Practice and the Architecture of the Mind*. London: Karnac Books.

Langs, R. (1996). *The Evolution of the Emotion-Processing Mind: With an Introduction to Mental Darwinism*. London: Karnac Books.

Langs, R. (1997). *Death Anxiety and Clinical Practice*. London: Karnac Books.

Langs, R. (Ed.) (1998). *Current Theories of Psychoanalysis*. Madison, CT: International Universities Press.

Langs, R., Badalamenti, A., & Thomson, L. (1996). *The Cosmic Circle*. Brooklyn, NY: Alliance.

LeDoux, J. (1996). *The Emotional Brain*. New York: Simon & Schuster.

Lieberman, P. (1991). *Uniquely Human*. Cambridge, MA: Harvard University Press.

Plutchik, R. (1993). Emotions and their vicissitudes: emotions and psychopathology. In M. Lewis & J. Haviland (Eds.), *Handbook of Emotions* (pp. 53–65). New York: Guilford Press.

Prigogine, I., & Stengers, I. (1984). *Order Out of Chaos*. New York: Bantam Books.

Weiss, J., & Sampson, H. (1986). *The Psychoanalytic Process: Theory, Clinical Observation, and Empirical Research*. New York: Guilford Press.

INDEX